THEIR HEARTS WERE YOUNG AND GAY

Other books by Marc Best

Those Endearing Young Charms

THEIR HEARTS WERE YOUNG AND GAY

Marc Best

South Brunswick and New York: *A. S. Barnes and Company*
London: *Thomas Yoseloff Ltd*

© 1975 by A. S. Barnes and Co., Inc.

A. S. Barnes and Co., Inc.
Cranbury, New Jersey 08512

Thomas Yoseloff Ltd
108 New Bond Street
London W1Y OQX, England

Library of Congress Cataloging in Publication Data

Best, Marc, 1948–
  Their hearts were young and gay.

  1. Moving-picture actors and actresses—United States—Biography.
  2. Children as actors. I. Title.
PN1998.A2B43   791.43′028′0922 [B]   74-9287
ISBN 0-498-01512-2

PRINTED IN THE UNITED STATES OF AMERICA

*To my Aunt Julia,
with everlasting love
and
eternal gratitude*

CONTENTS

Preface   9
Acknowledgments   11
Lee Aaker   15
Bennie Bartlett   22
Scotty Beckett   28
Bobby Blake (Little Beaver)   35
Bobby Breen   43
Billy Burrud   49
Butch and Buddy   55
Jackie Coogan   64
Virginia Lee Corbin   72
Frankie Darrow   78
Patty Duke   84
Madge Evans   91
Pamelyn Ferdin   97
Mimi Gibson   105
Bonita Granville   112
Billy Gray   119
Gary Gray   125
Darla Hood   131
Ra Hould   137
Claude Jarman, Jr.   143
Gloria Jean   150
Dickie Jones   155
Terry Kilburn   162
Mark Lester   169

Jerry Mathers (The Beaver)   175
The Mauch Twins   181
Jackie Moran   188
Danny Mummert   194
Donald O'Connor   201
Dawn O'Day   207
Patsy Lee Parsons   212
Luana Patten   218
Baby Peggy   223
Juanita Quigley (Baby Jane)   228
Michel Ray   234
Gene Reynolds   240
Larry Simms (Baby Dumpling)   247
Elizabeth Taylor   253
Rex Thompson   259
Ann Todd   265

PREFACE

Today's child performer is in a vastly different situation than were the children who jaunted across the screen in the Shirley Temple days. In those early years there existed an influx of movie moppets brought on by the film studios who sought to offset 20th Century-Fox's grosses by developing a Miss Temple of their own. Needless to say, this idea never did materialize. However, in the all-out effort to produce another "superbaby star," the studios continued making pictures in which youngsters were predominantly featured. Family films nearly always occupied the screen—the Bumsteads, Joneses, Peppers, and many others were shown in ever increasing abundance. They were simple productions at best, but they afforded a haven for the child actor that lasted until just a few years ago.

In 1946 television came into being. By 1950 and thereafter the small screen was gradually accepted into homes throughout America. This development served to radically change the movie industry. Family fare that at one time was exhibited in movie theaters could now be seen on television in the comfort of one's home. Theaters began to lose much of their adult patronage and those who did come expected to see entertainment that was both stimulating and mind challenging. Younger people desired movies of social significance.

This situation has forced the little stars of the celluloid to seek new employ on the small screen. Television, with its strict code of approval, continues to show features in which children are utilized. Let us hope that today's changing moral values do not envelop the television industry; if this should happen, a charming and endearing breed of movie performer may vanish for all time.

I was encouraged to write this sequel to *Those Endearing Young*

Charms through the wonderful letters received from readers, including one from Mrs. Sybil Drake, alias Sybil Jason, one-time Warner Brothers' child star.

In closing, I would like to congratulate two moppets whose recent performances were truly outstanding—Dawn Lyn in *Shoot Out* and Tatum O'Neal in *Paper Moon*. I hope that their portrayals will spur the motion picture industry to once again feature the little ones. Bring back the thirties! It truly was a memorable era.

ACKNOWLEDGMENTS

The author wishes to express his appreciation to the individuals and organizations listed below for their assistance in helping to make this book possible:

THE INDIVIDUALS:

Gene Andrewski, Ernest Corneau, Bill Gray, Paula Klaw, and Dorothy Day Otis.

THE ORGANIZATIONS:

ABC TV, Academy of Motion Picture Arts and Sciences, Bennett's Book Store, Bond Street Book Shop, Boston Public Library, Cherokee Book Store, Cinemabilia, Harvard Theatre Collection, Larry Edmunds Books, Library of the Performing Arts, Memory Shop, Museum of Modern Art, Photo Archives, Robbins Public Library, and the Silent Movie Theater.

WITH SPECIAL THANKS TO:

Miss Pamelyn Ferdin for a most memorable and rewarding interview.

THEIR HEARTS WERE YOUNG AND GAY

LEE AAKER

BORN: September 25, 1943. PLACE OF BIRTH: Inglewood, California. HAIR: Blond. EYES: Blue.

At the age of four Lee Aaker enrolled in a dancing school in Inglewood. Lee's mother, who was the school's instructress, obtained an engagement for him at the Orpheum Theater in Los Angeles. The role, a song-and-dance routine, came in December of 1948, but it was not his first professional assignment. This occurred a year earlier when he had a bit part in the film *The Governor of Louisiana,* portraying a member of the household.

In 1950 Lee received his first major role and it called for his enactment of a little, crippled boy in a Los Angeles hospital. Entitled *Benjy,* the film was based on the factual account of a youngster's existence in an orthopedic ward and was made when Lee was six years old. Two years later he became a Critics Award winner for his performance in *The Atomic City* (8).

Lee can also be seen in these movies: *No Room for the Groom* (8),* *O. Henry's Full House* (8), *The Desperate Search* (9), *Jeopardy* (9), *Take Me To Town* (9), *Arena* (9), *Hondo* (10), *Ricochet Romance* (11), *Destry* (11).

On television he appeared in *Letter To Loretta* (10), "Ford Theater" (10), "Fireside Theatre" (10), "Mr. and Mrs. North" (11), and "Director's Playhouse" (12). He had a leading role in the children's series "The Adventures of Rin Tin Tin" (10-14).

Lee received an education through private tutors and at the Wil-

---
* These numbers refer to the age of the performer when he appeared in each credit.

liam Kelsoe Elementary School in Inglewood. Football was his favorite sport.

In 1955 the youngster was the recipient of the Milky Way Gold Star Award as one of the nation's twelve most talented child performers. He also won the Critics Award for the 1953 film *Hondo* and gave one of the top five performances by a juvenile actor for that year.

The Atomic City
(Paramount, 1952)

In this picture Lee played a Los Alamos physicist's son who is kidnapped by a group of murderous spies. Gene Barry was seen as the physicist.

No Room for the Groom
(Universal, 1952)

Lee starred opposite Tony Curtis in this lighthearted comedy of a newly wed groom and his tedious honeymoon in a house filled with unwanted relatives.

Take Me to Town
(Universal, 1953)

Ann Sheridan, a convicted criminal, escapes on her way to the penitentiary and strives to win her way into a lumberjack's home. Sterling Hayden portrayed the woodsman, while Lee Aaker was seen as one of his three children.

Hondo
(Warner Brothers, 1953)

In this picture John Wayne appeared as an Indian scout, while Geraldine Page starred as a frontierwoman tending a ranch in Apache territory. Lee Aaker portrayed Miss Page's son, Johnny.

Ricochet Romance
(Universal, 1954)

Lee played the young son of a dude-ranch proprietor (Chill Wills). Marjorie Main was seen as the family cook.

BENNIE BARTLETT

BORN: August 16, 1927. PLACE OF BIRTH: Independence, Kansas. HAIR: Red. EYES: Blue.

Freckle-faced Bennie Bartlett started his show business career when he toured the Midwestern States in a play called *Foolish Wives*. Bennie's parents were members of the troupe and their son, at the age of four months, had the infant part in the production. Bennie learned to play the trumpet at the age of three; two years later he was singing with a dance orchestra. Next he appeared on the radio playing the trumpet and singing tunes that he had composed. One of these tunes, "You're Wonderful," was written by Bennie in honor of his mother's wedding anniversary. The youngster was the son of Nina and Floyd Bartlett, musicians.

In 1934 the family moved to the West Coast where they settled in Venice, California. Mr. Bartlett soon found a job arranging dance music for the local radio stations and he was able to get his son an audition at one of the networks. As a result of his singing and dancing talents, Paramount Pictures signed the boy to a contract in 1935 and used him in thirteen major productions.

His movie roles were: *Millions In the Air* (8), *Timothy's Quest* (8), *The Sky Parade* (8), *13 Hours By Air* (8), *The Texas Rangers* (8), *Three Married Men* (9), *Maid of Salem* (9), *Time Out for Romance* (9), *Let Them Live!* (9), *Exclusive* (9), *Danger—Love At Work* (10), *Bulldog Drummond's Revenge* (10), *Penrod and His Twin Brother* (10), *Berth Quakes* (10), *Sons of the Legion* (11), *Just Around the Corner* (11), *Gang Bullets* (11), *The Great Man Votes* (11), *The Family Next Door* (11), *What a Life* (12), *Honeymoon In Bali* (12), *Our Neighbors, the Carters* (12), *Alias the*

Deacon (12), *Let's Make Music* (13), *Meet John Doe* (13), *Tillie The Toiler* (13), and *Code of the Outlaw* (14).

Bennie's favorite hobby was playing with model trains.

As an adult performer, Bennie Bartlett made numerous film appearances. He was cast as one of the original Bowery Boys in eighteen productions for Monogram Pictures and Allied Artists between 1949 and 1955.

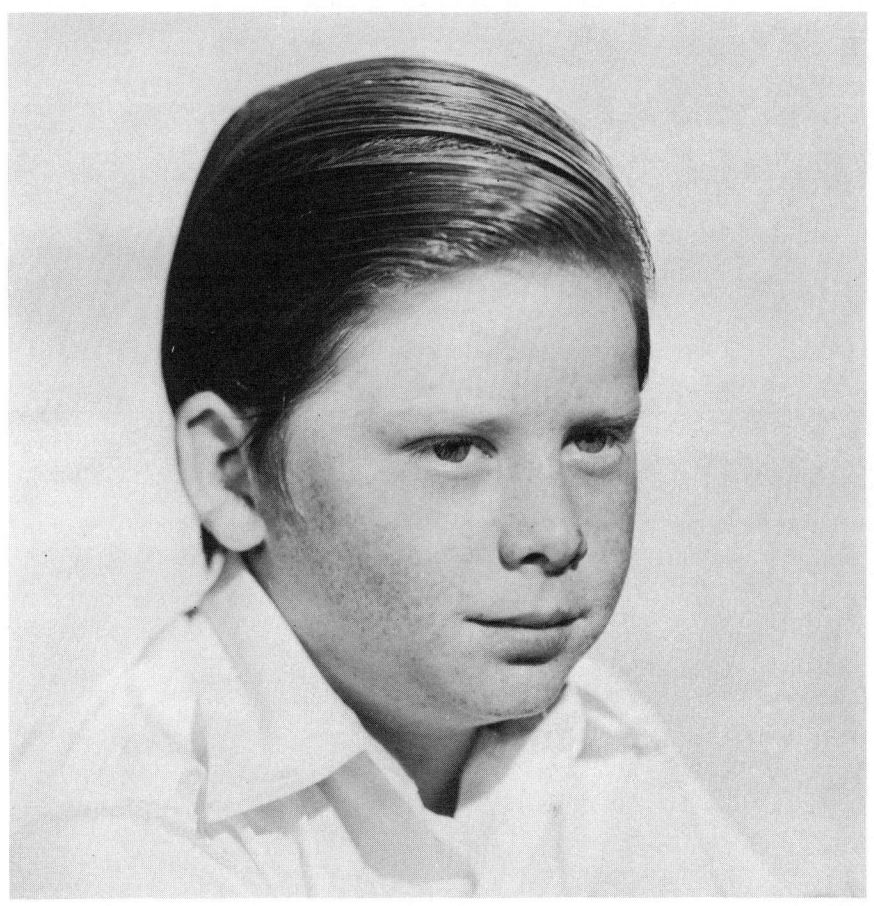

Time Out for Romance
(20th Century-Fox, 1937)

Bennie co-starred in this picture with Joan Davis and William Demarest. Claire Trevor appeared in the lead role as a runaway heiress.

Danger—Love At Work
(20th Century-Fox, 1937)

Otto Preminger directed this film about a zany family named Pemberton. Bennie appeared as Junior, a ten-year-old prodigy who spreads chaos throughout the household. Bennie is shown here with co-star Jack Haley.

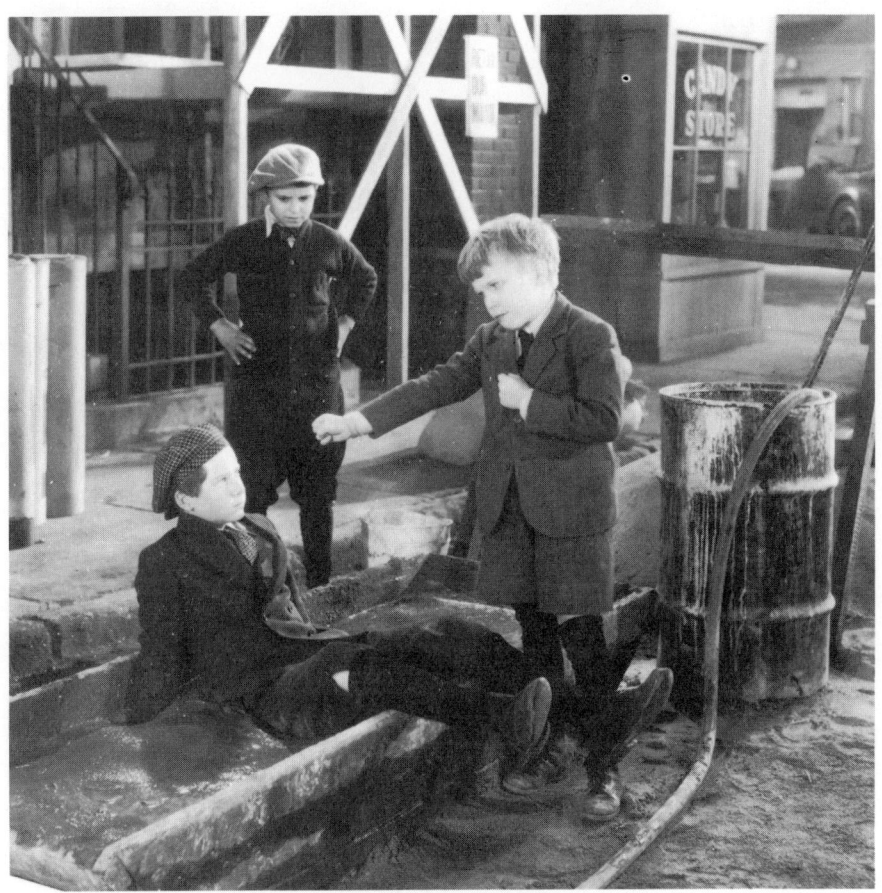

The Great Man Votes
(RKO Radio, 1939)

For this film Bennie was seen as a school bully. In this scene he receives his just deserts by Peter Holden, who played the son of the town drunk (John Barrymore).

The Family Next Door
(Universal, 1939)

This picture had Ruth Donnelly and Hugh Herbert as the fun-loving Mr. and Mrs. Pierce. Bennie was seen in the part of Rufus, their cantankerous twelve-year-old son.

Our Neighbors, the Carters
(Paramount, 1939)

When a large drug chain forces the town druggist out of business, his family has trouble making ends meet. Bennie was seen as Junior Carter, while Frank Craven portrayed the luckless druggist, "Doc" Carter. Also pictured are Joyce Arleen and Gloria Carter.

SCOTTY BECKETT

BORN: October 4, 1929. PLACE OF BIRTH: Oakland, California. HAIR: Brown. EYES: Brown.

When Scotty was three, he moved with his family from Oakland to Los Angeles, California. A year later his father became ill and the little boy spent considerable time at the hospital amusing his dad by singing several of the more popular tunes of the day. On one of his visits to the hospital, Scotty was noticed by a motion-picture casting director and then given a screen test. When it proved noteworthy, Scotty registered with Central Casting and soon he was called to do a bit part in United Artists' *Gallant Lady*. Pleased by Scotty's ability to convey emotion, 20th Century-Fox used him for a bit part in *Stand Up and Cheer*. Three months later, in July of 1934, he completed his first major role in Columbia's *Whom the Gods Destroy*.

Hal Roach, producer of *Our Gang*, interviewed Scotty in January of 1934 and signed him to a five-year contract. Someone at the Roach Studios had the idea of teaming Scotty with "Spanky" McFarland, since they were approximately the same age and the youngest members of the "Gang." The result was a hilarious group of shorts that extended over a two-year period. Scotty became familiar to audiences as the little boy in oversized turtleneck sweater and trousers, and the bearer of a cap that he wore bent over the side of his head.

Scotty Beckett performed in seventeen *Our Gang* productions. His first comedy was *Mike Fright* (4), and this was followed by featured roles in *Hi, Neighbor* (4), *Washee Ironee* (4), *Little Papa* (5), and *Cousin Wilbur* (9). Scotty's finest role came in the short, *The First Round-Up* (4), in which he and Spanky were two baby campers who showed up the older "Gang" members on a week's camping trip.

Scotty's reign with Hal Roach was not an unusually lengthy one. Eventually he was phased out by "Alfalfa" Switzer who replaced him as Spanky's sidekick. Beginning in April of 1936, Scotty departed from the Roach lot and concentrated his efforts in doing motion pictures. However, he did make two guest appearances with the "Gang" in 1939 when he was seen as Alfalfa's cousin.

His movie assignments were: *Whom the Gods Destroy* (4), *Dante's Inferno* (5), *Pursuit* (5), *I Dream Too Much* (6), *The Case Against Mrs. Ames* (6), *Anthony Adverse* (6), *The Charge of the Light Brigade* (6), *Life Begins With Love* (7), *Conquest* (7), *The Bad Man of Brimstone* (8), *The Devil's Party* (8), *Marie Antoinette* (8), *Four's a Crowd* (8), *Listen, Darling* (8), *The Flying Irishman* (9), *Blind Alibi* (9), *Mickey the Kid* (9), *Our Neighbors, the Carters* (9), *The Escape* (10), *Days of Jesse James* (10), *The Blue Bird* (10), *My Son, My Son* (10), *My Favorite Wife* (10), *Street of Memories* (10), *Gold Rush Maisie* (10), *Father's Son* (11), *Aloma of the South Seas* (11), *The Vanishing Virginian* (12), *Kings Row* (12), *It Happened In Flatbush* (12), *Between Us Girls* (12), *The Youngest Profession* (13), *Good Luck, Mr. Yates* (13), *Ali Baba and the Forty Thieves* (14), *The Climax* (14).

From 1945 to 1950, Scotty Beckett handled over a dozen film assignments. His career then began to rapidly decline and for the next six years he was seen in only four pictures. After several years of no film work and some personal misfortunes, Scotty entered a rest home in Hollywood on May 8, 1968. Two days later he was found dead in bed. Pills and a note were found in his room, but the note did not provide any concrete explanation for his death.

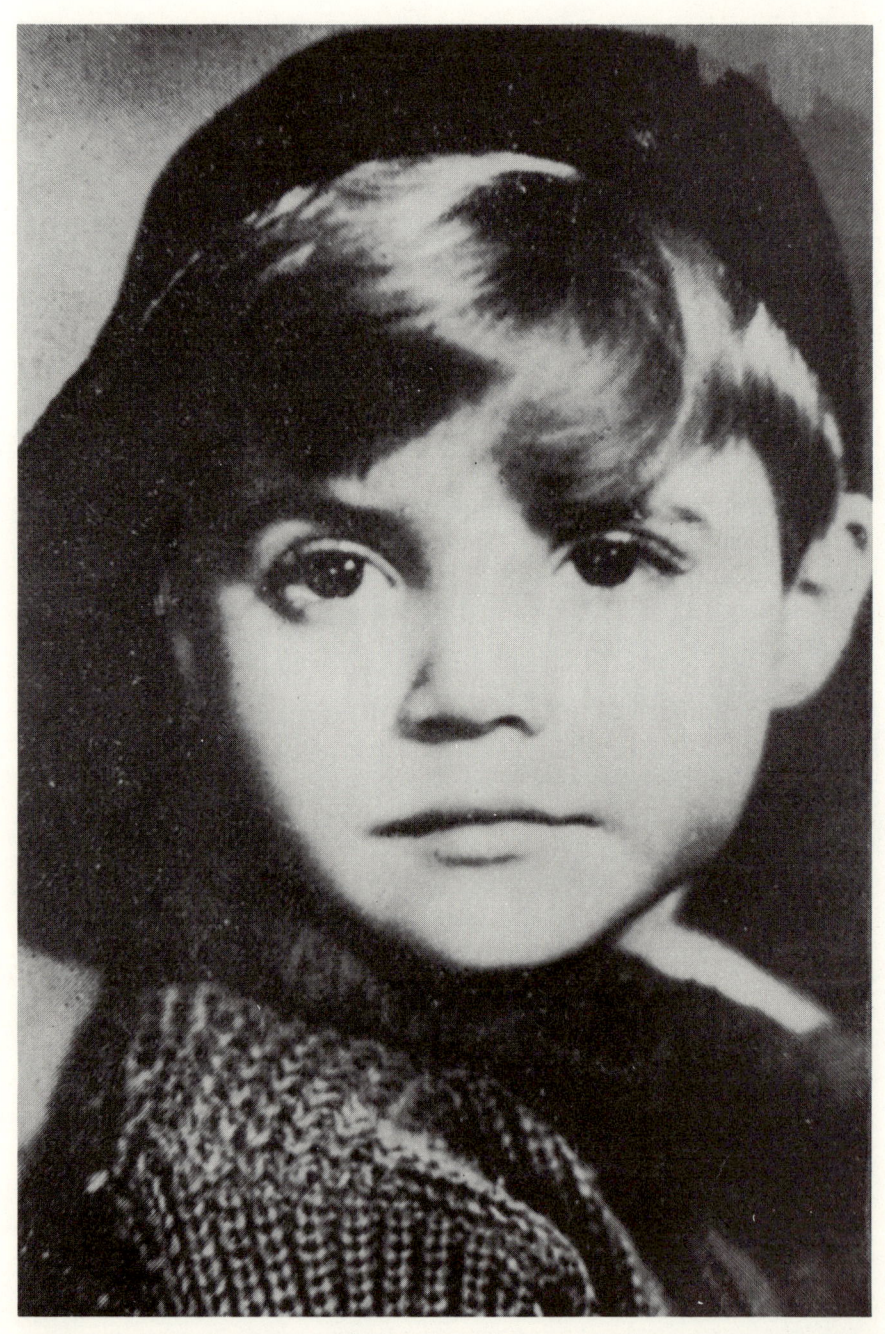

Whom the Gods Destroy
(Columbia Pictures, 1934)

Scotty Beckett and Walter Connolly were son and father in this Walter Lang feature.

The Case Against Mrs. Ames
(Paramount, 1936)

Following the death of her playboy husband, a woman clashes with in-laws over the custody of her son, Bobby. Madeleine Carroll and Scotty Beckett appeared as mother and son.

Our Neighbors, the Carters
(Paramount, 1939)

Scotty was seen as one of five children belonging to "Doc" Carter (Frank Craven) a druggist in a small Midwestern town.

My Son, My Son
(United Artists, 1940)

In this film Scotty had the role of Brian Aherne's son, Oliver. Madeleine Carroll also starred.

My Favorite Wife
(RKO Radio, 1940)

This comedy-feature relates the story of a woman who returns to her husband and two children after being stranded on a desert island for seven years. Irene Dunne and Cary Grant were the principals. Scotty played their son, Tim.

BOBBY BLAKE
(LITTLE BEAVER)

BORN: September 18, 1933. PLACE OF BIRTH: Nutley, New Jersey. HAIR: Brown. EYES: Brown.

Born Mickey Gubitosi in Nutley, New Jersey, Bobby Blake had the distinction of being starred in two highly popular film series —*Our Gang* and *Red Ryder*. Bobby's first *Our Gang* comedy role was in *Joy Scouts* at the age of five. Cast as Mickey, he was usually portrayed as a melancholy little boy who delivered every line with a whine in his voice. In all, Bobby Blake performed in forty comedies. Probably his finest performances came in: *Dad For a Day* (6), *Goin' Fishin'* (7), *Baby Blues* (7), and *Farm Hands* (9).

In the early part of 1943, Spanky and Alfalfa had out-grown their roles and this placed Bobby as the leading "Gang" member. He held this position until late in 1944 when MGM decided to curtail production of the shorts. *Dancing Romeo* (10) was Bobby's final assignment and the last of the *Our Gang* features.

In May of 1944, Bobby adopted the nickname of "Little Beaver," as he was cast in a film series based upon the exploits of the comic-strip cowboy, Red Ryder. William Elliott held the title role for sixteen episodes, while Bobby enacted the part of Little Beaver, Ryder's sidekick, a total of twenty-three times and he was seen in every episode.

He had parts in these movies: *Mokey* (8), *Andy Hardy's Double Life* (9), *China Girl* (9), *Lost Angel* (10), *Marshal of Reno* (10), *Tucson Raiders* (10), *The San Antonio Kid* (10), *Cheyenne Wildcat* (10), *The Big Noise* (10), *The Woman In the Window*

(10), *Vigilantes of Dodge City* (11), *The Sheriff of Las Vegas* (11), *The Great Stagecoach Robbery* (11), *The Horn Blows At Midnight* (11), *Pillow to Post* (11), *Phantom of the Plains* (11), *The Marshal of Laredo* (11), *Dakota* (12), *Colorado Pioneers* (12), *Lone Texas Ranger* (12), *Wagon Wheels Westward* (12), *California Gold Rush* (12), *A Guy Could Change* (12), *The Sheriff of Redwood Valley* (12), *Sun Valley Cyclone* (12), *Conquest of Cheyenne* (12), *In Old Sacramento* (12), *Home On the Range* (12), *Sante Fe Uprising* (12), *Out California Way* (13), *Humoresque* (13), *Stagecoach To Denver* (13), *Homesteaders of Paradise Valley* (13), *Vigilantes of Boomtown* (13), *Oregon Trail Scouts* (13), *The Marshal of Cripple Creek* (13), *Rustlers of Devil's Canyon* (13), *The Last Round-Up* (13), *The Return of Rin Tin Tin* (14), *The Treasure of the Sierra Madre* (14).

With over seventy-five film appearances to his credit, Bobby Blake ranks high on Hollywood's list of most active child performers. His twenty-eight assignments for Republic Pictures are the most any youngster has accumulated for an individual studio. In addition to his Western roles, Bobby was used in many dramatic films like *Mokey* and *The Treasure of the Sierra Madre*.

Bobby acted steadily during the fifties and sixties. As Robert Blake, he's had some important roles in pictures over the past six years, with his best achievements coming in *In Cold Blood* (1967) and *Tell Them Willie Boy Is Here* (1969).

Mokey
(Metro-Goldwyn-Mayer, 1942)

Bobby had the title role in this film. He portrayed a mischievous, nine-year-old youngster who causes undue hardships for his father and newly acquired stepmother.

The Woman in the Window
(RKO Radio, 1944)

Fritz Lang directed this mystery-melodrama that starred Edward G. Robinson as a psychology professor who gets entangled in murder. Bobby was seen as Robinson's young son.

The Horn Blows at Midnight
(Warner Brothers, 1945)

Jack Benny starred in this fanciful comedy about a radio-band trumpeter who, during a commercial break, falls asleep and dreams he's an angel sent to earth to sound the crack of doom. Bobby played a cantankerous little imp named Junior.

Oregon Trail Scouts
(Republic, 1947)

This episode from the Red Ryder features depicted how the hero (Allan Lane) formed his partnership with Little Beaver (Bobby Blake).

Treasure of the Sierra Madre
(Warner Brothers, 1948)

John Huston directed this film that starred Humphrey Bogart as a gold prospector. Bobby appeared as a Mexican boy.

BOBBY BREEN

BORN: November 4, 1927. PLACE OF BIRTH: Toronto, Canada. HAIR: Light brown. EYES: Dark brown.

Bobby Breen was the son of musically talented parents and he had three siblings who were also musically inclined. His sister, Sally, achieved prosperity in musical comedies as a singer-dancer and it was she who introduced Bobby to Miss DeMonterey, a voice instructress. The teacher was quick to take note of the boy's talent and she personally aided in his voice development.

When he was four years old, Bobby made his professional debut at Toronto's Silver Slipper Night Club. He sang at the club for two years; he made numerous radio appearances, and received bookings on the vaudeville stage in Toronto. Later, Bobby was given engagements at the Oriental Theatre in Chicago, Illinois, and the Gotham and Paramount Theaters in New York City.

Bobby's long awaited break arrived when he performed a comedy skit entitled *Say When* at the Professional Children's School. It was this role that enabled the youngster to secure a position on the "Eddie Cantor Show" on the radio. He was on the program for two seasons and became nationally known as Cantor's "adopted son of the air."

Following his stay with Cantor, Bobby entered films. He began by enrolling as a pupil of Mario Marafioti, voice instructor to famous opera stars. Sol Lesser, a producer for RKO Radio Pictures, heard the boy sing an aria from *Rigoletto* and had him placed under contract at a starting salary of $75 a week. By late 1939 the "male Shirley Temple" had been starred in eight RKO productions and his salary had increased to $350 a week.

He debuted in *Let's Sing Again* (8) and followed this with major roles in *Rainbow On the River* (8), *Make a Wish* (9), *Hawaii Calls* (10), *Breaking the Ice* (10), *Fisherman's Wharf* (11), *Way Down South* (11), and *Escape To Paradise* (12).

Bobby was an avid baseball enthusiast and an excellent swimmer.

After World War II, Bobby spent some time in the real-estate business. In 1961 he was back in show business when the Thunderbird Recording Company of Miami Beach, Florida, signed him to a recording contract. Today, Bobby appears in nightclubs around the world and his Bobby Breen Productions arranges bookings for him in such faraway locations as New Zealand and South Africa.

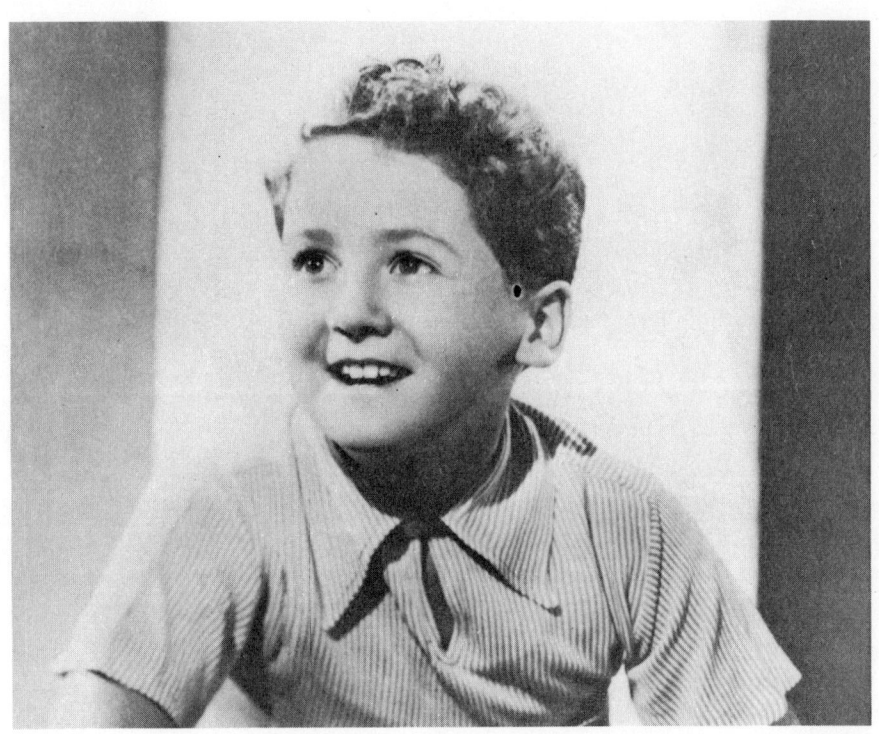

Let's Sing Again
(RKO Radio, 1936)

Bobby appeared as a runaway orphan who joins a traveling show managed by a kindly Italian (Henry Armetta).

Rainbow on the River
(RKO Radio, 1936)

Bobby had the main role as a post-Civil War southern boy who is forced to live with his stuffy New York grandmother and a number of designing cousins.

Make A Wish
(RKO Radio, 1937)

Bobby was seen as Chip, a youngster attending a boys' camp in Maine. Bobby sings: "Music in My Heart," "My Campfire Dreams," and "Polly Wolly Doodle."

Hawaii Calls
(RKO Radio, 1938)

Bobby, as an orphan-stowaway on a Hawaiian-bound steamship, gets involved in spy activities. His songs include "Down Where the Trade Winds Blow" and the title song, "Hawaii Calls."

Fisherman's Wharf
(RKO Radio, 1939)

In this Sol Lesser production, Bobby played a youngster who runs away from home upon discovering that he is only an adopted son. Leo Carrillo was also featured.

BILLY BURRUD

BORN: January 12, 1925. PLACE OF BIRTH: Hollywood, California. HAIR: Light brown. EYES: Blue.

Billy's first acting assignments came in Little Theater productions at the Hollywood Community Theater School. At the age of nine, he received considerable attention through his performance in *Music In the Air,* which played the circuits in Los Angeles and San Francisco. Various movie studios took notice and the boy was offered some choice roles in pictures. Universal furnished the most substantial part in *Three Kids and a Queen,* so Billy signed a seven-year contract with the studio.

His other film assignments were: *His Night Out* (10), *Pride of the Marines* (11), *The Cowboy and the Kid* (11), *Two In a Crowd* (11), *Postal Inspector* (11), *The Magnificent Brute* (11), *Girl Overboard* (12), *Fair Warning* (12), *Captains Courageous* (12), *The Man in Blue* (12), *Idol of the Crowds* (12), *It Happened in Hollywood* (12), *Night Hawk* (13).

In 1936, following his performance in *Pride of the Marines,* Billy Burrud became the youngest honorary member of the U.S. Marine Corps, and life-size pictures of him in uniform were hung at the headquarters building in San Diego.

He was educated at the Hollywood Community Theater School and enjoyed swimming, horseback riding, and baseball.

In 1954 Billy Burrud founded the Bill Burrud Enterprises, which produced such syndicated features as "Wanderlust," "Islands In the Sun," "The American West," and "True Adventure." Bill was given a shot at network television in June of 1969 when he became host-narrator of "Animal Kingdom," a wildlife-action-adventure program on NBC. His latest achievements have been as the host-narrator of "Animal World" on CBS and as the narrator of the Kal Kan pet-food commercials.

Three Kids and a Queen
(Universal, 1935)

May Robson had the lead role in this film about an eccentric old woman who is "adopted" by a group of Hell's Kitchen youngsters. Billy appeared as "Doc."

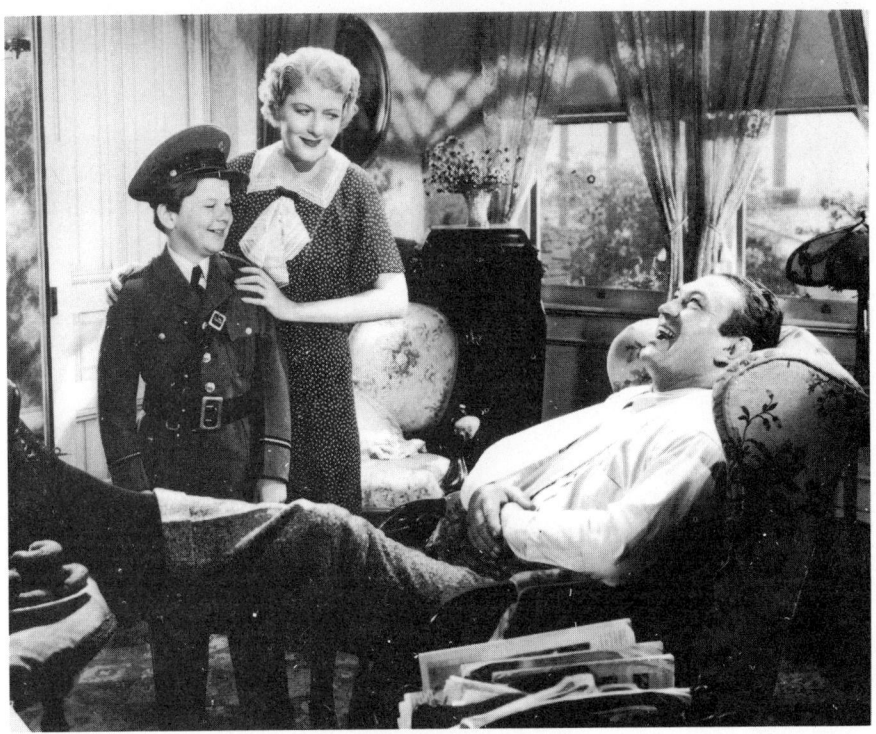

The Magnificent Brute
(Universal, 1936)

Billy played the son of a widowed, boardinghouse proprietor. Jean Dixon starred as the widow, while Victor McLaglen portrayed Big Steve Andrews, a steel-mill bully whom the youngster hero-worships.

Fair Warning
(20th Century-Fox, 1937)

Billy starred in this mystery-comedy opposite Betty Furness and John Payne. The story concerns a series of murders that occur at a Death Valley winter resort.

Captains Courageous
(Metro-Goldwyn-Mayer, 1937)

Freddie Bartholomew had the lead role as a spoiled, rich kid who falls off a liner bound for Europe and is rescued by a Portuguese fisherman (Spencer Tracy). Billy portrayed a young bully who had a row with master Bartholomew aboard ship.

Idols of the Crowds
(Universal, 1937)

Billy was seen with John Wayne in this hokey drama.

BUTCH AND BUDDY

BUTCH

BORN: December 14, 1930. PLACE OF BIRTH: Edmond, Oklahoma.
HAIR: Brown. EYES: Blue.

Billy Lenhart—Butch of Butch and Buddy—began playing the bass fiddle when he was just three years old. Not long afterwards, Billy joined his older brother in a radio act that was aired over the networks in Oklahoma City. Billy's parents brought him to Hollywood on the advice of a film scout, but the youngster soon found himself on the vaudeville stage after numerous unsuccessful auditions at several movie studios. This vaudeville stint took him through the better part of twenty states and his act consisted of playing the fiddle and performing a few dance numbers. (See As A Team)

His screen credits are: *Sandy Is a Lady* (9), *Spring Parade* (9), *A Little Bit of Heaven* (9), *In the Navy* (10), *Never Give a Sucker An Even Break* (10), *Man From Montana* (10), *Melody Lane* (10), *Johnny Doughboy* (11), *Cinderella Swings It* (12), *Spotlight Scandals* (12), *A Lady Takes a Chance* (12), *Army Wives* (13).

BUDDY

BORN: January 20, 1932. PLACE OF BIRTH: Baltimore, Maryland.
HAIR: Blond. EYES: Blue.

Kenneth Brown—Buddy of Butch and Buddy—began playing the accordion at the age of four. Known as the "show-stopper of Baltimore," little Kenneth Brown gave his first performance accompanied by the U.S. Navy Band on NBC radio. He also made appearances on the "Major Bowes Amateur Show" and at Baltimore's Century Theater. His ability to play the accordion was so outstanding, the Peabody Conservatory of Music in Baltimore awarded him a scholarship in 1937.

In addition to playing the accordion, Kenny could also handle himself well on the piano. He attended a public school in the San Fernando Valley. (See As A Team)

His movie credits are: *Sandy Is a Lady* (8), *Spring Parade* (8), *A Little Bit of Heaven* (8), *In the Navy* (9), *Never Give a Sucker An Even Break* (9), *Man From Montana* (9), *Melody Lane* (9), *Johnny Doughboy* (10), *Cinderella Swings It* (10), *Bomber's Moon* (11), *Spotlight Scandals* (11), *A Lady Takes a Chance* (11), *Army Wives* (12).

AS A TEAM

In October of 1938, Butch and Buddy were called for separate auditions at a studio. While waiting in the hall to be interviewed, the boys strummed a little duet. It was then that they decided to join forces, with their first assignments coming in vaudeville shows and Hollywood benefits. Late in 1939 the youngsters scored well at the press review of Universal's *The Under-Pup*, were signed to term contracts, and emerged as an outstanding musical comedy team. They made a dozen films together and did not break up the act until 1943 when Buddy made *Bomber's Moon* for 20th Century-Fox.

Butch

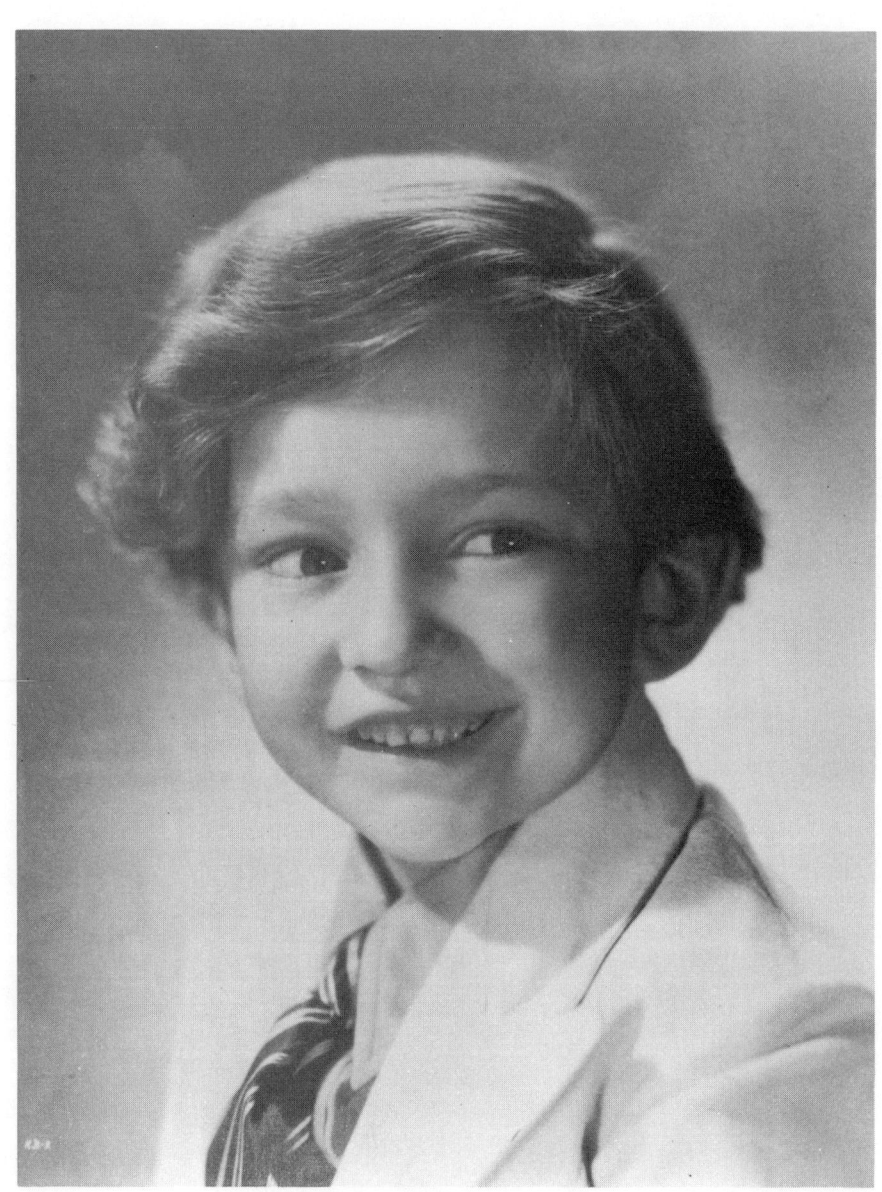
Buddy

Spring Parade
(Universal, 1940)

Deanna Durbin had the lead role in this musical tale of Old Vienna, with S. Z. Sakall appearing as a lovable old baker and Butch and Buddy starring as his helpers.

A Little Bit of Heaven
(Universal, 1940)

Butch and Buddy appeared in this rags-to-riches musical-romance opposite an all-star cast headed by Hugh Herbert, Billy Gilbert (in picture), and C. Aubrey Smith.

Never Give a Sucker an Even Break
(Universal, 1941)

W. C. Fields headed the cast of this comedy film, while Butch and Buddy were seen as two precocious lads who heckle him to distraction.

Melody Lane
(Universal, 1941)
Butch and Buddy starred in this musical production under the direction of Charles Lamont.

Cinderella Swings It
(RKO Radio, 1943)

Butch and Buddy starred opposite Guy Kibbee in this adaptation of the Scattergood Baines stories by Clarence Kelland. The boys add considerable merriment to the proceedings concerning a young concert singer (Gloria Warren) whose career suddenly blossoms when she adopts the swing style.

JACKIE COOGAN

BORN: October 26, 1914. PLACE OF BIRTH: Los Angeles, California. HAIR: Blond. EYES: Brown.

Vaudeville and Jackie Coogan were born almost simultaneously. Both of Jackie's parents were vaudevillians; his father was a comedian while his mother was a singer-dancer. At the age of eighteen months, Jackie began to exhibit a talent for mimicry and could give an amusing imitation of filmstar David Warfield. In the summer of 1916, the boy made his first acting appearance and it came before a sell-out crowd at New York's Riverside Theatre. Towards the end of the matinee performance, Jackie crawled on stage from the wings and sat grinning at the audience. Jackie's father, who was on stage at the time, persuaded his son to give the Warfield imitation and the patrons brought the house down. From then on Jackie was a frequent partner in his parents' act.

In April of 1919 Jackie and his parents were booked at the Orpheum in Los Angeles. Sid Grauman, owner of Grauman's Chinese Theater, happened to witness the youngster's imitations that, as usual, were the hit of the act. Grauman knew that Charlie Chaplin was attempting to locate a prospective child for the title role in *The Kid,* so he brought Chaplin to the theater. The comic hadn't been seated more than two minutes before he stood up and stared in amazement. Chaplin was so enthralled with Jackie's antics that he had him signed to a contract the following evening.

Kid was the turning point in Jackie's acting career, for he then went on to star in fourteen motion pictures for First National and Metro Studios. He was one of the top ten money-making stars of 1924 and had earned upwards of $500,000 by early 1925.

He made appearances in the following films: *A Day's Pleasure* (5), *The Kid* (6), *Peck's Bad Boy* (6), *My Boy* (7), *Trouble* (7), *Oliver Twist* (7), *Daddy* (8), *Circus Days* (8), *Long Live the King* (8), *A Boy of Flanders* (9), *Little Robinson Crusoe* (9), *The Rag Man* (10), *Old Clothes* (10), *Johnny Get Your Hair Cut* (12), *The Bugle Call* (12), *Buttons* (13).

At the age of fourteen Jackie toured Europe, visiting such cities as Berlin, Vienna, London, and Paris. In Paris he and his father gave a repartee at the Empire Music Hall. Jackie, appearing in top-hat and white spats, recited a humorous piece, sang a little tune, and briskly performed a few dance numbers.

Jackie attended the Los Angeles Military Academy when he was thirteen, but prior to this he was educated by private tutors. His pastimes were swimming and playing baseball.

As a juvenile performer, Jackie Coogan was cast in *Tom Sawyer* and *Huckleberry Finn*. Later he acted in *The Joker Is Wild* (1957), *Lonelyhearts* (1959), and *The Shakiest Gun In the West* (1968). One of his most recent releases was an NBC World Premiere movie entitled *Cool Million* in which he had a cameo role as a movie director. He also appeared as Uncle Fester in television's "The Addams Family."

The Kid
(First National, 1920)

Jackie, Charlie Chaplin, and Edna Purviance were the featured players in this comedy about the warmhearted relationship between a crusty derelict and an abandoned youngster.

Oliver Twist
(First National, 1922)

Jackie Coogan was seen as Oliver in this second movie presentation of the Charles Dickens novel.

Daddy
(First National, 1923)

Jackie had a field day in this film of an eight-year-old boy and his friendship with an old street fiddler.

Long Live the King
(Metro, 1923)

Jackie was seen in this film as a young monarch named Otto, heir apparent to the throne of the Kingdom of Libernia.

Old Clothes
(Metro-Goldwyn, 1925)

Jackie Coogan and Max Davidson were partners in a junk business with Jackie playing the levelheaded businessman and Max portraying a lovable loser. Joan Crawford, in only her second motion picture, was seen as a lonely destitute who is befriended by the two and taken into their home.

VIRGINIA LEE CORBIN

BORN: December 5, 1910. PLACE OF BIRTH: Prescott, Arizona. HAIR: Blonde. EYES: Big and blue.

At the age of three, Virginia Lee Corbin was engaged as a model for a professional artist. A year later she undertook a film career with the Balboa Feature Film Company, but her assignments for the studio were quite incidental. In late 1917 Virginia's acting career blossomed as she became leading lady of the famous Fox "Kiddie" Classics. Her first performance was *Jack and the Beanstalk* (6), and this was followed shortly thereafter by *Aladdin and the Wonderful Lamp* (6), *Babes In the Woods* (6), *Treasure Island* (7), *Fan Fan* (7), and *Ali Baba and the Forty Thieves* (7).

Her other films were: *The Chorus Girl and the Kid* (5), *Six Shooter Andy* (7), *Ace High* (7), *The Forbidden Room* (8), *Scrambled Wives* (10), *Beyond the Rainbow* (11), *Destiny's Isle* (11), *Wine of Youth* (13), *Sinners In Silk* (13), *The City That Never Sleeps* (13), *Broken Laws* (13).

In addition to her movie work, Virginia Lee gave many singing and dancing performances at society functions within the Los Angeles area. She also toured the RKO vaudeville circuit during the summer of 1921, when she sang, danced, and performed impersonations. Known as "the Shirley Temple of the Silent Era," Virginia Lee Corbin made approximately one million dollars before her fourteenth birthday.

Her pastimes consisted of playing the ukelele, taking classical dancing lessons, and playing with dolls. She was educated in the Hollywood public schools.

In 1929 Virginia Lee retired from motion pictures following a number of successful years as a "flapper." Eight years later she was employed as a coach for aspiring models. On June 4, 1942 the former star died of a lengthy heart ailment. She was only thirty-one years of age.

Jack and the Beanstalk
(20th Century-Fox, 1917)

Virginia Lee Corbin had the role of Princess Regina in this picture.

Jack and the Beanstalk
(20th Century-Fox, 1917)

In this adaptation of the well-known fairy tale, Jack (Francis Carpenter) kills the evil giant and wins the hand of the fair maiden (Virginia Lee).

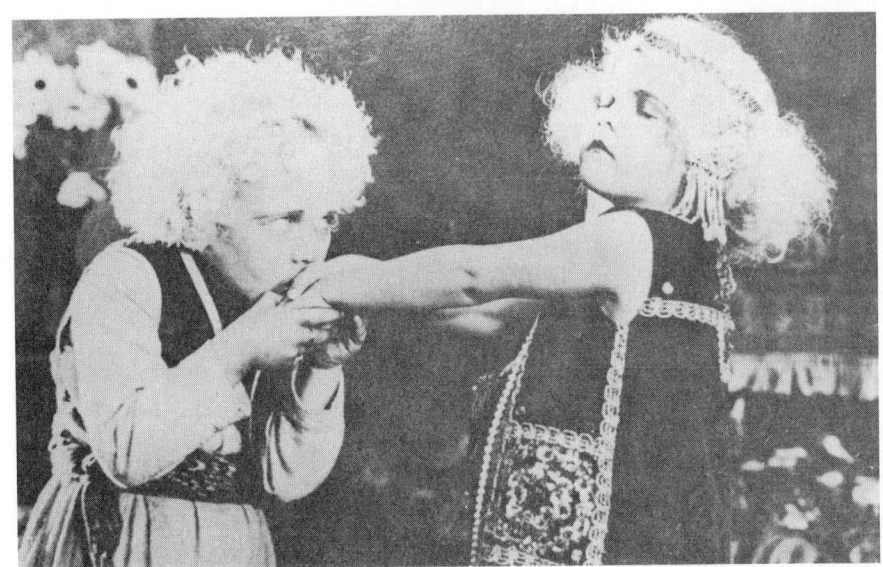

Aladdin and the Wonderful Lamp
(20th Century-Fox, 1917)

Virginia Lee's part in this picture closely resembled Theda Bara's *Cleopatra,* for she dressed in flowing robes and took baths in luxurious pools.

Fan Fan
(20th Century-Fox, 1918)

Virginia Lee portrayed a winsome Japanese girl in this final "Kiddee" classic. The film was based on the Gilbert and Sullivan operetta, *The Mikado.*

The City That Never Sleeps
(Paramount, 1924)

As Molly, Virginia Lee played a young girl who was brought up in the not-so-glorious atmosphere of a bustling saloon.

FRANKIE DARROW

BORN: December 22, 1917. PLACE OF BIRTH: Chicago, Illinois. HAIR: Dark brown.

Serious, solemn-faced Frankie Darrow, who was christened Frank Johnson, made his professional debut before a live audience. Frankie's parents were members of a vaudeville act on the Orpheum and Pantages circuits in Chicago, and the youngster's first taste of show business came when he took bows on stage with his family. The boy's vaudeville stay was a short one, however, as Hollywood beckoned him to perform a leading role in the 1923 Metro-Goldwyn feature *Half-a-Dollar Bill*. He then free-lanced in films until 1926 when the Film Booking Offices issued him a contract.

Frankie was used in a score of cowboy pictures by the FBO Studios in which he acted opposite their leading Western hero, Tom Tyler. Although Frankie was used predominantly in Westerns, he did manage to perform well in straight roles for films like *Little Mickey Grogan* and *The Rainbow Man*.

He received his education through private tutors both at home and in between takes on the set.

His film assignments were: *Half-a-Dollar Bill* (5), *Signal Tower* (6), *Roaring Rails* (6), *So Big* (6), *Confessions of a Queen* (7), *Her Husband's Secret* (7), *Fearless Lover* (7), *Fighting Flames* (7), *Wandering Footsteps* (7), *Phantom Express* (7), *Mike* (8), *Memory Lane* (8), *Kiki* (8), *Hearts and Spangles* (8), *The Carnival Girl* (8), *The Cowboy Cop* (8), *Out of the West* (8), *Tom and His Pals* (8), *Her Father Said No* (8), *Lightning Lariats* (9), *Long Pants* (9), *Moulders of Men* (9), *Cyclone of the Range* (9), *Judgment of the Hills* (9), *Flying U Ranch* (9), *The Desert Pirate* (9),

The Texas Tornado (10), *Little Mickey Grogan* (10), *Phantom of the Range* (10), *When the Law Rides* (10), *The Circus Kid* (10), *Terror Mountain* (10), *The Avenging Rider* (10), *The Tyrant of Red Gulch* (10), *Trail of the Horse Thieves* (11), *Gun Law* (11), *The Rainbow Man* (11), *The Red Sword* (11), *Idaho Red* (11), *The Pride of Pawnee* (11), *Blaze O'Glory* (11), *The Vanishing Legion* (13), *Lightning Warrior* (13), *The Mad Genius* (13), *Cheyenne Cyclone* (13), *Way Back Home* (14), *Amateur Daddy* (14), *The Devil Horse* (14), *Three On a Match* (14).

As he grew older, Frankie Darrow was cast in tough-guy roles in such films as *Reformatory* and *Juvenile Court*. He made a few pictures with the Bowery Boys in the late forties and ended his career with *Operation Petticoat* in 1959.

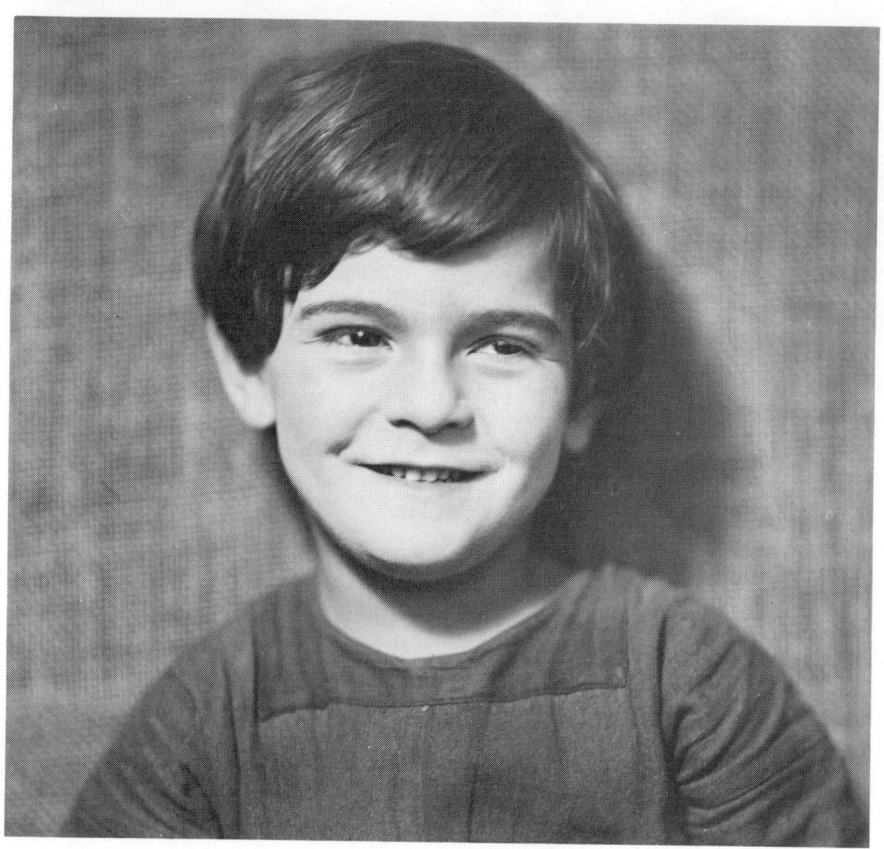

Half-a-Dollar Bill
(Metro-Goldwyn, 1923)

Frankie had the title role appearing as a foundling who is raised by the captain of a sailing vessel. The film deals with the lad's adventures aboard ship, and also starred William Carlton as the captain.

The Signal Tower
(Universal, 1924)

In this feature, one of Clarence Brown's earliest directing efforts, Frankie was seen as the son of Rockcliffe Fellows, a railroad signalman.

The Desert Pirate
(Film Booking Offices, 1927)

The Circus Kid
(Film Booking Offices, 1928)

Frankie Darrow, as Buddy, played an orphan boy who runs away from school to join a circus. Joe E. Brown, seen here with Frankie, had the role of the circus lion tamer.

The Rainbow Man
(Paramount, 1929)

For this production, Frankie is adopted by a minstrel singer named Rainbow Ryan (Eddie Dowling).

PATTY DUKE

BORN: December 14, 1946. PLACE OF BIRTH: New York City. HAIR: Honey blond. EYES: Blue green.

Patty Duke, born Anna Marie Duke to Irish-American parents, lived the first eight years of her life in New York's East Side. As a little girl Patty loved to dress up and pretend, so it was not surprising that she should harbor thoughts of becoming an actress when she was only six years old. Patty's thirteen-year-old brother, Raymond, was then appearing in television commercials and the moppet decided that she too wanted to become a celebrity.

Patty's first professional assignment was a nonspeaking one. It came late in 1955 on television's "Voice of Firestone" and Patty was used in a short dance sequence. At the age of nine she was handed her first speaking part, appearing as an Italian waif in the "Armstrong Circle Theater" presentation of the sinking of the Andrea Doria. In 1957 Patty landed her first film role when she and her brother enacted a pair of foster children in the documentary entitled *The Deep Well.*

Early in 1958 John Ross, an actor's coach, began Patty's training for the role of Helen Keller. She learned how to master the unfocused stare of the blind and was shown how to disregard any sudden or loud noises. After ten grueling months, Patty had mastered her role to perfection. When auditions for *The Miracle Worker* began, Patty was so well prepared that she won the part easily. The play, which ran for a year and a half and 700 performances on Broadway, starred Patty as Helen Keller in every show up to the final five weeks.

Her motion picture credits are: *The Goddess* (11), *Country Mu-*

sic Holiday (11), 4-D Man (12), Happy Anniversary (12). On the stage she was seen in *The Miracle Worker* (12-14).

Patty has had over forty television assignments. They included several appearances in the soap operas "Kitty Foyle" and "The Brighter Day" and guest shots on programs such as: "The Paul Winchell Show," The Phil Silvers Show," and "The Frankie Laine Show." Her other roles were in *Swiss Family Robinson* (11), *Wuthering Heights* (11), *One Red Rose for Christmas* (11), *Family Happiness* (12), *Meet Me In St. Louis* (12), and *Zone of Silence* (12).

In January of 1960 Patty Duke was made cover girl of *Theatre Arts Magazine*. Two months later, at the age of thirteen, Patty became the youngest actress ever to be starred on Broadway when her name was raised above the title of the play *The Miracle Worker*. At the peak of her success in the specified play, Patty Duke was earning a salary of $30,000. She received the Theatre World Award as Most Promising Personality for 1959-1960.

Patty attended the Sacred Heart of Jesus and Mary School and the Willard Mace School for Professional Children. Her pastimes consisted of roller skating, swimming, and reading books on history.

As an adult performer, Patty Duke acted in the film version of *The Miracle Worker* and won an Academy Award as Best Supporting Actress. She had her own series on television from 1963 through 1966, "The Patty Duke Show." Patty can also be seen in *Valley of the Dolls* (1967), *Me Natalie* (1969), and *My Sweet Charlie* (1970). In 1972 she appeared in the ABC Movie of the Week entitled *Deadly Harvest*. As of this writing, Patty's new motion picture, *You'll Like My Mother*, was being exhibited in theaters around the country.

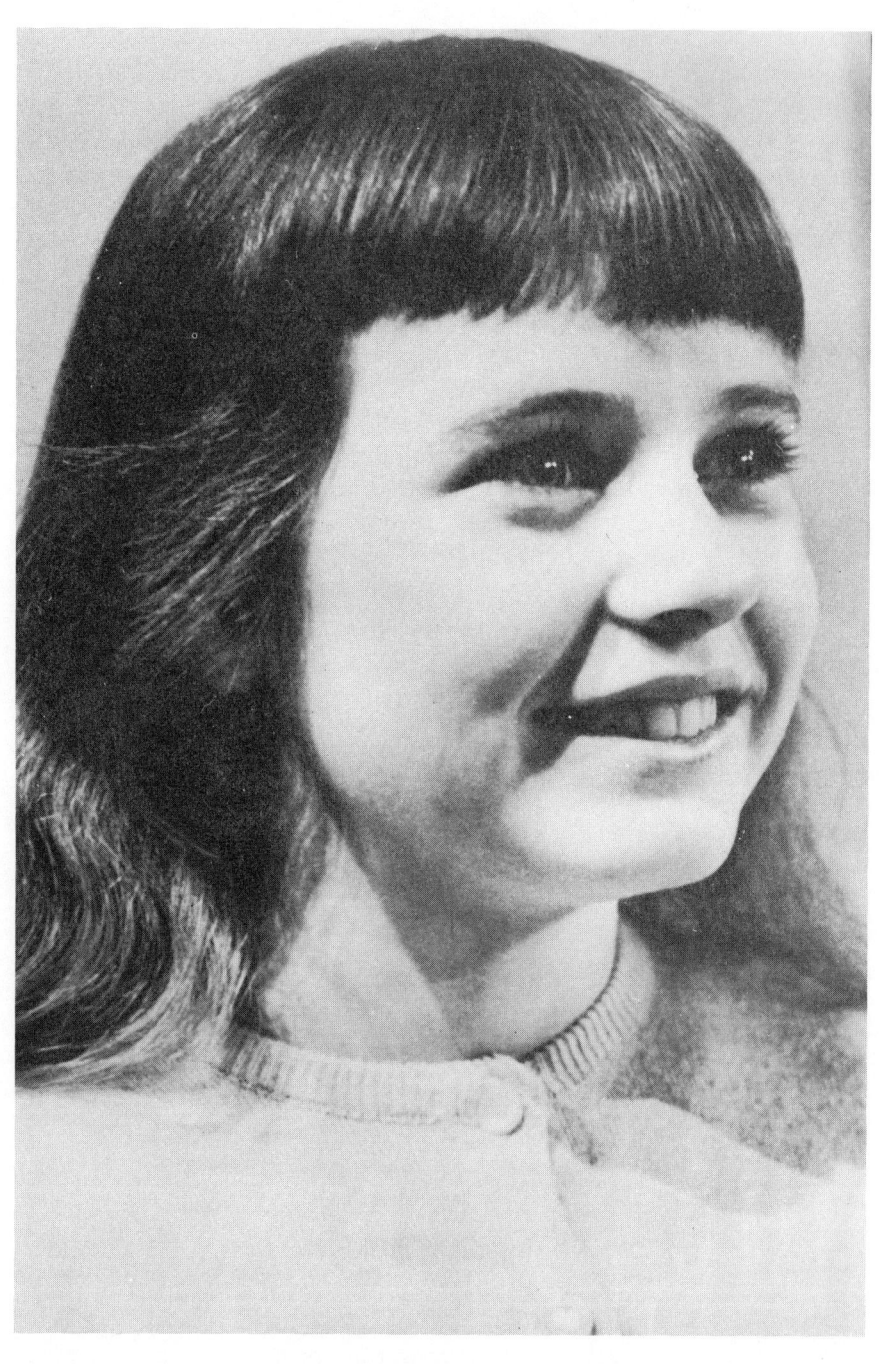

One Red Rose for Christmas
(CBS TV, 1958)

In this "U. S. Steel Hour" drama presentation, Patty acted opposite the leading lady of the theater, Helen Hayes.

4-D Man
(Universal, 1959)

Patty had a co-starring role in this science-fiction thriller about a man who has the power to pass through solid matter. Lee Meriwether was also featured.

Happy Anniversary
(United Artists, 1959)

Young Debbie Walters (Patty) creates pandemonium in her home when she discloses a family scandal on television. Mitzi Gaynor and David Niven played the frustrated parents.

The Miracle Worker
(New York Stage Play, 1959)

On October 19, 1959, at the Playhouse Theatre on Broadway, Patty Duke starred as Helen Keller, a deaf mute, who was taught how to communicate by a persevering teacher named Annie Sullivan (Anne Bancroft). This is the final act of the play when little Helen suddenly comprehends the meaning behind the "touch language."

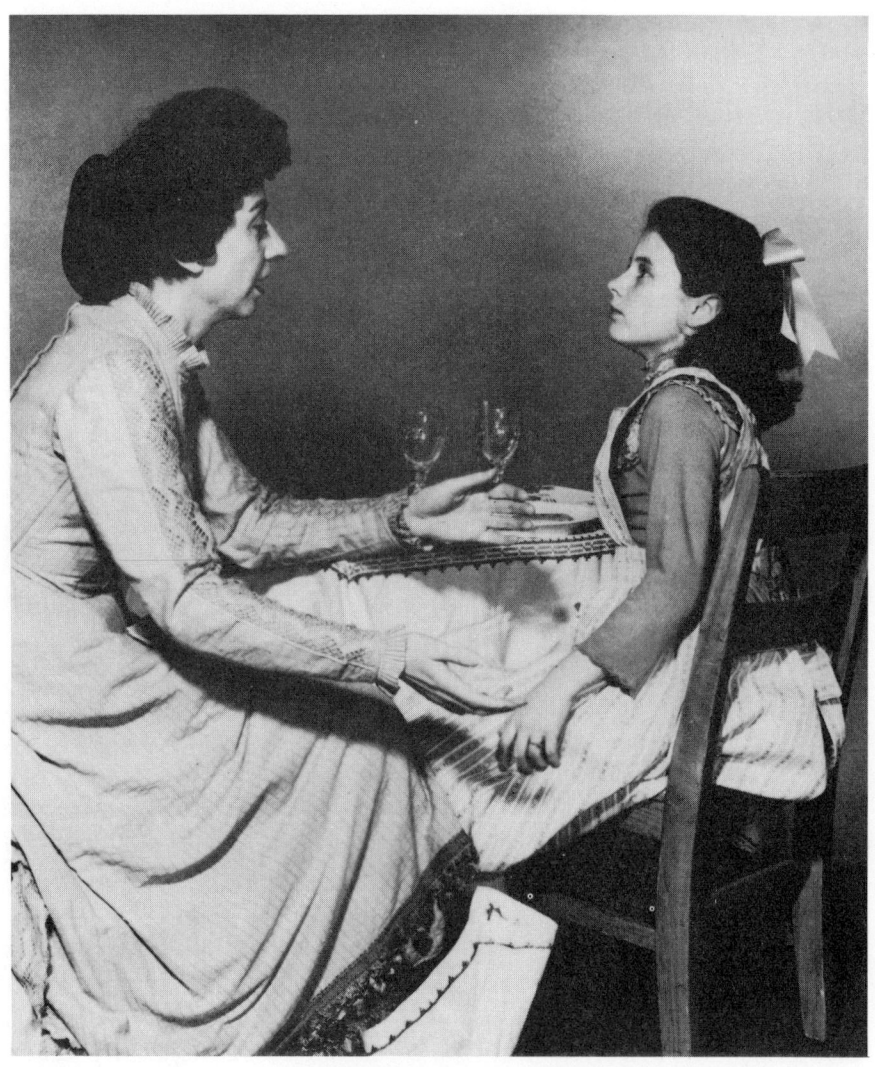

The Miracle Worker
(New York Stage Play, 1959)

In this scene spoiled and pampered Helen is at the dinner table where she has just defiantly dropped her napkin for the second time.

MADGE EVANS

BORN: July 1, 1909. PLACE OF BIRTH: New York City. HAIR: Blond. EYES: Big and blue.

Madge Evans was born only a few months after her parents arrived in New York from Liverpool, England. At the age of eight months Madge was posing for a Madonna and Child painting; at twelve months she was engaged as the laughing model for the *Baby Book*.

Known as the "loveliest baby in America," Madge began to acquire recognition in 1914 when she and her older brother were hired to advertise cracked wheat and baby food. As time wore on, little Madge established herself as "child queen of the models" with New York's finest commercial artists. Her face could be seen on portrait paintings, sculpture, post cards, calendars, posters, and fashion plates.

In 1915 the moppet undertook a film career obtaining a minor role in Universal's *Garden of Lies*. Eleven months later, she was placed under contract by World Pictures following her acclaimed performance in *Sudden Riches*. Madge went on to star in over a dozen pictures for the Peerless-Brady-World Studios and she accomplished this within a span of only four years.

Even though she was an extremely active movie performer, Madge still found time to pursue her modeling career. Late in 1918 she was seen trying on the current hat fashions in some of New York's leading department stores, and she was also able to pose as Cupid for the sculptor F. S. Church.

As pastimes Madge enjoyed playing with dolls and stuffed animals. Her education was via private tutors.

On the screen the youngster appeared in *Alias Jimmy Valentine* (5), *Seven Sisters* (5), *Zaza* (6), *The Little Church Around the Corner* (6), *Sudden Riches* (6), *Husband and Wife* (7), *Hidden Scar* (7), *Seventeen* (7), *Web of Desire* (7), *Maternity* (7), *The Beloved Adventuress* (7), *The Little Duchess* (8), *The Corner Grocer* (8), *The Adventures of Carol* (8), *The Burglar* (8), *The Volunteer* (8), *Woman and Wife* (8), *Gates of Gladness* (8), *Wanted—A Mother* (8), *Stolen Orders* (8), *Neighbors* (9), *Love Net* (9), *The Love Defender* (9), and *Home Wanted* (9).

In addition to her movie assignments, Madge had a two-month stay on Broadway in *Peter Ibbetson* (7).

Madge Evans appeared in more than thirty motion pictures as an adult performer beginning with *Lovers Courageous* in 1932 and finishing with *Army Girl* in 1938.

Husband and Wife
(Brady-World, 1916)

Husband and Wife
(Brady-World, 1916)

Madge starred alongside Ethel Clayton and Holbrook Blinn.

The Corner Grocer
(Paramount, 1917)

The Adventures of Carol
(World Films, 1917)

Madge appeared as a youngster whose goodness straightens out the tangled lives of two stubborn grandparents.

The Volunteer
(World Films, 1917)

In this film Madge was the daughter of an Army officer. The story deals with the relationship existing between the little girl and her Quaker grandparents during the First World War.

PAMELYN FERDIN

BORN: February 4, 1959. PLACE OF BIRTH: Los Angeles, California. HAIR: Dark blond. EYES: Blue.

Pamelyn's earliest acting performance came at the age of three when she received a part in a Christmas play entitled *Oh, Christmas Tree* at the Chateau Drama Theater. A year later Pam began to accompany her acting sisters, Wendy and Valerie, on visits to the studios. Shortly thereafter, the youngster was tested for a Clairol television commercial, which she won in competition against twenty-five other applicants.

In 1964, following a year of commercial work, Pamelyn appeared in a bit role for the 20th Century-Fox film *What a Way To Go*. Although the part was a minor one, it proved to be a fine stepping-stone for future assignments in *The One and Only, Genuine, Original Family Band* (7), *Guess What I Did Today?* (7), *Daughter of the Mind* (9), *The Christine Jorgenson Story* (10), *The Mephisto Waltz* (10), *The Beguiled* (10), *What's the Matter With Helen?* (11), *The Forgotten Man* (12), and *Happy Birthday, Wanda June* (12).

On television Pamelyn made guest appearances in "The Littlest Hobo" (5), "Jesse James" (6), "Death Valley Days" (6), "Branded" (6), "Family Affair" (7), "Gunsmoke" (8), "Star Trek" (8), "The Flying Nun" (8, 9), "Walt Disney's Wonderful World of Color" (9), "High Chaparral" (9), "Mannix" (11), "The Odd Couple" (12), "Night Gallery" (12), "Marcus Welby, M.D." (12), "Love, American Style" (12), "Lassie" (12), and "Young Dr. Kildare" (13). Her series performances have been: "The John Forsythe Show" (6), "Blondie" (8), "Curiosity Shop" (12), "Lassie" (13), "The Paul Lynde Show" (13).

Besides acting, Pam has had many roles that required her to give voice impressions. She was Lucy in "It Was a Short Summer, Charlie Brown" (9), "A Boy Named Charlie Brown" (10), "You're In Love, Charlie Brown" (12); Fern in the motion picture *Charlotte's Web* (13); Percocia in the television cartoon series "Roman Holidays" (13), and Lilibit in the ABC Superstar Movie presentation of *Oliver and the Artful Dodger* (13).

In 1968 the little girl received the Critics Award from *Film Daily*, honoring her performance in *The One and Only, Genuine, Original Family Band*. Three years later she was an Emmy Award nominee for her role in the "Marcus Welby" production of *A Portrait of Debbie*. One of Pamelyn's most cherished moments came shortly after completion of the above assignment when she received a testimonial letter from the star of "Marcus Welby"—Robert Young.

On many occasions Pam's roles have called for her to sing and dance. Early in her career she was given dancing parts on "The Danny Kaye Show" (6), "The Andy Williams Show" (6), and "The Jerry Lewis Show" (9). She undertook dancing lessons at the age of three and a half by enrolling in the Gilbert's Theatrical Dancing Studio; ten years later Pam was dancing in a benefit show in honor of Busby Berkeley.

In 1967, at the age of eight, Pamelyn made three singing appearances on "The Woody Woodbury Show." In 1970 she sang a couple of tunes in a "Yes-In" at the Hollywood Bowl, and the following year she sang and strummed the guitar as a regular on "Curiosity Shop."

Quite active outside the studio sets, Pam can ski, play tennis, swim, ride horseback, cook, sew, and compose songs. Her favorite pastime, however, is walking her dalmatian dog, Tabathena. She has been educated at the Franklin Elementary School, the Los Feliz Elementary School, and the Le Conte Junior High.

Pamelyn Ferdin is a truly dedicated young performer. She seeks to make acting her profession and hopes to attend the UCLA Drama School immediately upon graduation from high school.

The One and Only, Genuine, Original Family Band
(Buena Vista, 1967)

This Disney feature starred Walter Brennan as the leader of a family band that he hopes will be asked to perform at the 1888 Democratic Convention in St. Louis. Pamelyn was featured as Laura Bowen (center, light dress), one of Brennan's eight grandchildren. In this scene the band rehearses the campaign song "Let's Put It Over With Grover."

The Mephisto Waltz
(20th Century-Fox, 1971)

Pamelyn was seen as Abby Clarkson, a youngster who dies as a result of Satanism.

The Beguiled
(Universal, 1971)

Pamelyn was seen in this film as a little girl named Amy. The picture relates her deep fondness for a Union soldier whom she finds lying near death in the woods. Clint Eastwood starred as the soldier.

"Marcus Welby, M. D."
(ABC TV, 1972)

Following the death of their daughter, a couple adopt an eleven-year old girl. Pamelyn starred as the foster child, Felicia.

"The Paul Lynde Show"
(ABC TV, 1973)

Sally (Pamelyn) leaves home in this episode after she is forbidden to see her boyfriend, Jimmy.

MIMI GIBSON

BORN: 1948. PLACE OF BIRTH: Renton, Washington. HAIR: Blond. EYES: Blue.

In 1950, at the age of twenty-two months, Mimi Gibson embarked on a professional career by posing for calendars. A short time later the little girl became acquainted with Emerson and Theda Hall, well-known West Coast portrait photographers. Early in 1953 the Halls flew East with a vast library of photographs taken of Mimi in various poses. They circulated the pictures among the magazine houses and, in April, Mimi was hired by *American Magazine* to be their cover girl. A month later she completed her first major film role in *A Slight Case of Larceny*.

Larceny was Mimi's first starring role, but she actually made her movie debut back in January of 1951 when she recited two lines of dialogue in *Gasoline Alley* for Columbia Pictures. In addition to her natural beauty, Mimi's success in motion pictures was due to what her mother termed a "bear-trap mind," which enabled the moppet to recall her lines after only a couple of takes.

Mimi had parts in the following movies: *I'll See You In My Dreams* (3), *Everything I Have Is Yours* (4), *My Pal Gus* (4), *A Slight Case of Larceny* (4), *The Egyptian* (6), *There's No Business Like Show Business* (6), *The Bottom of the Bottle* (7), *Rebel In Town* (8), *Strange Intruder* (8), *Drango* (8), *Wings of Eagles* (8), *The Monster That Challenged the World* (8), *Courage of Black Beauty* (9), *The Three Faces of Eve* (9), *No Down Payment* (9), *Houseboat* (10), *The Buccaneer* (10), *The Remarkable Mr. Pennypacker* (10), and *I'll Give My Life* (10).

She made television guest appearances on "Four Star Playhouse" (6), "The Loretta Young Show" (6), "Climax" (7), "Jane Wyman Presents" (7, 8), "One Step Beyond" (10).

Besides acting, the youngster was adept at dancing and singing, and once cut a disc entitled "Sweetheart Time" with screen star Ray Middleton. Mimi won the Critics Award for her performance in *Houseboat* and was voted one of the top five juvenile actresses for 1958. Her favorite pastime was playing with dolls.

Drango
(United Artists, 1957)

Mimi had a brief but endearing role as an orphaned, Southern girl who is befriended by a Union soldier (Jeff Chandler).

The Wings of Eagles
(Metro-Goldwyn-Mayer, 1957)

John Ford directed this picture about naval hero Frank "Spig" Wead, casting John Wayne in the title role. Mimi was seen as his daughter, Lila; Maureen O'Hara appeared as the mother.

No Down Payment
(20th Century-Fox, 1957)

Mimi appeared with an all-star cast in this drama of life in a housing project. Joanne Woodward (in picture), Tony Randall, Jeffrey Hunter, and Barbara Rush starred as the heads of four neighboring families. In the film Mimi was seen as the daughter of Barbara Rush.

The Remarkable Mr. Pennypacker
(20th Century-Fox, 1959)

Mimi had the role of Elizabeth Pennypacker, one of seventeen children being raised by a free-thinking, self-made man named Horace Pennypacker, Jr. Clifton Webb was seen in the title role and Dorothy McGuire also appeared.

I'll Give My Life
(Howco International, 1959)

Mimi appeared with Ray Collins, who for many years portrayed Lieutenant Tragg on "Perry Mason."

BONITA GRANVILLE

BORN: February 2, 1923. PLACE OF BIRTH. New York City. HAIR: Curly blond. EYES: Blue.

Bonita Granville was the daughter of theatrical parents; Bernard Granville was a comedy star with the Ziegfeld Follies, while her mother, the former Rosina Timponi, was a stage performer. Mrs. Granville retired from show business in 1925 in order to devote full-time efforts towards coaching her daughter for a professional career.

In 1926 Bonita's father headlined his own vaudeville show and his daughter joined him one evening in a walk-on at New York's Palace Theater. A vaudeville swing in 1931 brought the girl to Hollywood, and a stark resemblance to film great Ann Harding caused a major film studio to cast her in *Westward Passage* (9). Charles Richards, an RKO casting director, gave the little girl a screen test, which she passed brilliantly. Bonita signed a $150-a-week contract, which was raised to $225 a week following her Academy Award nomination for *These Three* (12).

Her other screen roles were: *Cavalcade* (9), *Cradle Song* (10), *Ah, Wilderness* (12), *Song of the Saddle* (13), *The Plough and the Stars* (13), *Maid of Salem* (13), *Call It a Day* (13).

Bonita was educated on the studio sets and at the Le Conte Junior High. Her main recreation consisted of playing the piano.

As late as 1946, Bonita was seen performing in movies such as *The Truth About Murder* and *Love Laughs At Andy Hardy*. Her final assignment was in Warner Brother's *The Lone Ranger* in 1956. She co-produced television's "Lassie" program from 1958 to 1972.

Westward Passage
(RKO Radio, 1932)

Bonita, as Little Olivia, played a mischievous youngster who succeeds in making life quite hectic for her author-father. Sir Laurence Olivier starred as the frustrated parent, while Ann Harding played his wife.

Cavalcade
(20th Century-Fox, 1933)

This film told the story of an English family named Marryot and traces their growth for a thirty-year period from the Boer War to the First World War. Bonita was seen briefly in the picture's early sequences.

Ah, Wilderness
(Metro-Goldwyn-Mayer, 1935)

This film, adapted from the play by Eugene O'Neill, dealt with the hectic life of a high school senior just prior to his graduation. Eric Linden was cast in the main role, while Bonita Granville had the part of the younger sister, Mildred. Wallace Beery appeared as Uncle Sid.

These Three
(United Artists, 1936)

Bonita starred as a spiteful girl named Myra Tilford who spreads a lie that alters the lives of three innocent people. The film was directed by William Wyler and adapted from the Lillian Hellman play, *The Children's Hour*.

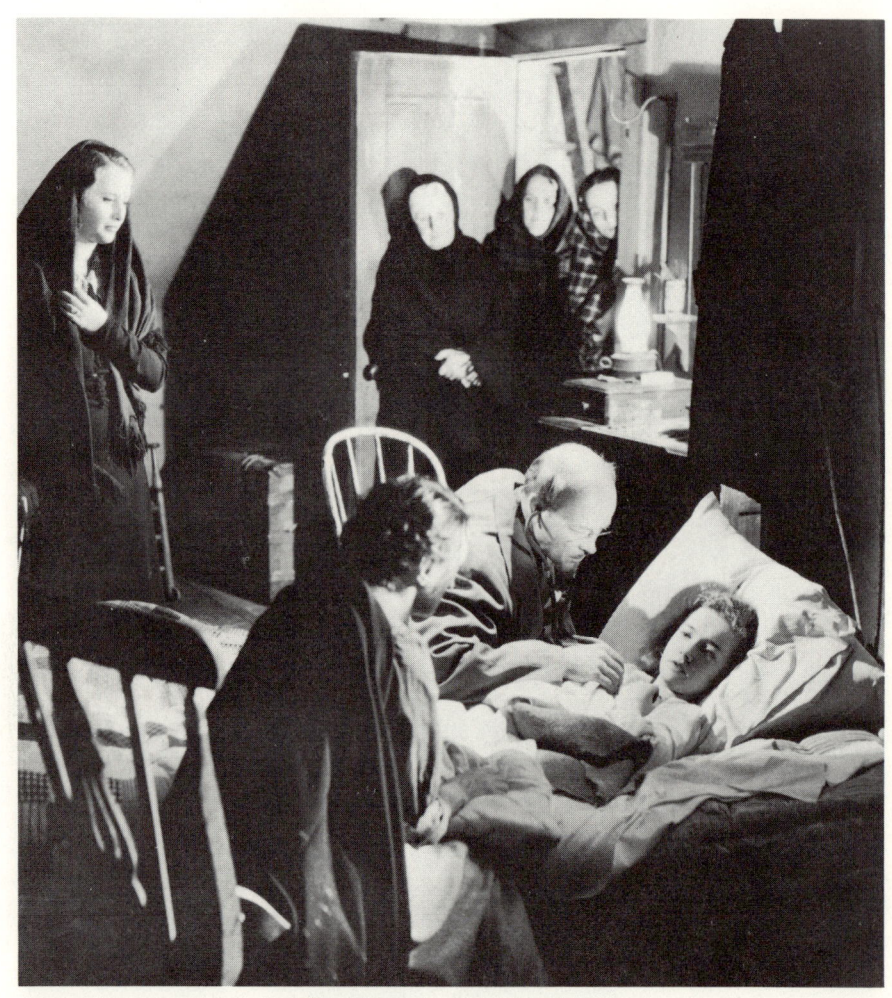

The Plough and the Stars
(RKO Radio, 1936)

Bonita appeared opposite Barbara Stanwyck and Barry Fitzgerald in this film of life in the Dublin slums during the 1916 Easter Rebellion. John Ford directed.

BILLY GRAY

BORN: January 13, 1938. PLACE OF BIRTH: Los Angeles, California. HAIR: Brown. EYES: Blue.

Billy Gray, son of character actress Beatrice Gray, started his film career quite by accident. One afternoon Billy went to see his brother Fred, perform in a play. At the theater he met his mother's agent, Lola Moore, and she asked him if he would like to be an actor. Billy was more than enthusiastic, so she arranged for him to go on interviews. From the interviews came his first role, an appearance in the *Nesbitt Passing Parade* short feature entitled *Our Old Car* (8).

Following his screen debut, Billy received some fine supporting roles in motion pictures. He earned top billing in 1951 with *The Guy Who Came Back* (13) and a few months later was a Critics Award winner for his performance in *The Day the Earth Stood Still* (13). He also had assignments in these films: *The Hal Roach Comedy Carnival* (9), *Fighting Father Dunne* (10), *Father Is a Bachelor* (12), *Sierra Passage* (12), *Singing Guns* (12), *Jim Thorpe—All American* (13), *On Moonlight Bay* (13), *Talk About a Stranger* (14), *The Return of Gilbert and Sullivan* (14).

On radio Billy had parts in *On Moonlight Bay* and *Room For One More* for the Lux Radio Theater.

Billy's education was acquired at St. Brendon's Parochial School, Emerson Junior High, and the 20th Century-Fox Studio School. The boy was an avid fisherman, an expert swimmer, and a fine water skier.

As an adult performer Bill Gray has had roles in features like *Some Like It Hot* (1959), *Two For the Seesaw* (1962), and *Dusty and Sweets McGee* (1971), but he is remembered most for his characterization of Bud Anderson in the CBS comedy series "Father Knows Best."

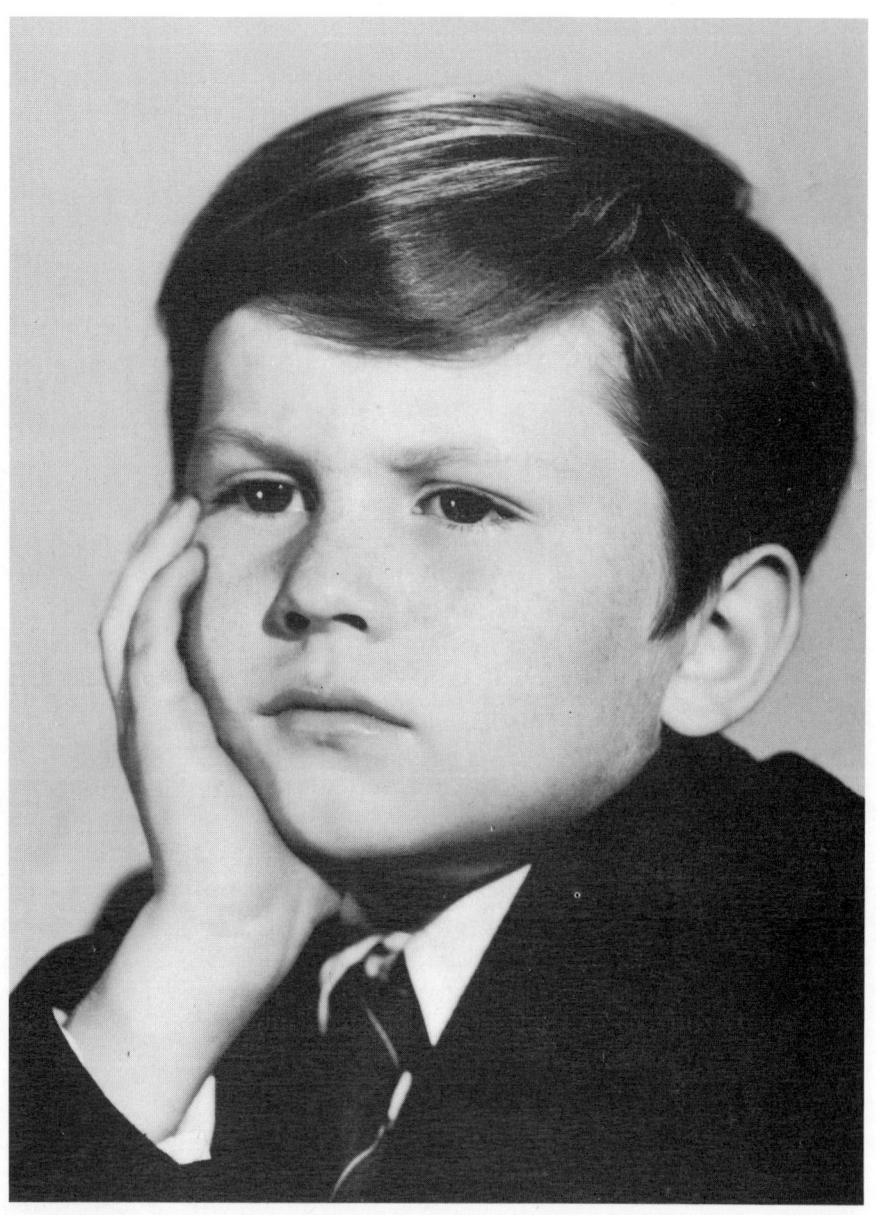

The Hal Roach Comedy Carnival
(United Artists, 1947)

Billy Gray was one of many featured players in this juvenile comedy; Frances Rafferty portrayed a rookie schoolteacher who, in this scene, uncovers the trickery of a young student (Billy).

Father Is a Bachelor
(Columbia Pictures, 1950)

William Holden starred in this film about a widower and his three children. Billy Gray, Mary Jane Saunders, and Gary Gray had the juvenile leads.

On Moonlight Bay
(Warner Brothers, 1951)

Doris Day had the principal role in this film as Marjorie Winfield, a blond tomboy who developed a crush on a college man. Billy portrayed her energetic younger brother. Leon Ames also appeared.

The Guy Who Came Back
(20th Century-Fox, 1951)

Paul Douglas performed the main role in this picture. He played an aging gridiron great who refuses to believe that his onetime prowess is now a thing of the past. Billy portrayed his loving son, Willy.

Talk About A Stranger
(Metro-Goldwyn-Mayer, 1952)

Billy Gray appeared as a youngster who suspects a newcomer in town of having poisoned his dog. Kurt Kasznar starred as the stranger.

GARY GRAY

BORN: December 18, 1936. PLACE OF BIRTH: Los Angeles, California. HAIR: Blonde. EYES: Blue.

Credit for Gary Gray's emergence into the film industry must be given to his father, William Gray, a onetime-motion-picture business manager. The elder Gray recognized his son's potential as an actor and obtained him a role in *A Woman's Face* at the age of four. In the film, Gary was called upon to smile at Joan Crawford, who enacted a facially disfigured woman. Viewing the completed picture, executives felt the impact of Gary's performance and awarded him roles of much greater significance. He earned star billing in August of 1948 with the release of RKO's *Rachel and the Stranger*.

On the screen the youngster appeared in *Address Unknown* (7), *The Adventures of Rusty* (8), *Rendezvous-24* (9), *The Best Man Wins* (11), *Return of the Badmen* (11), *Fighting Back* (11), *Rachel and the Stranger* (11), *The Night Wind* (11), *Gun Smugglers* (11), *Henry, the Rainmaker* (12), *The Streets of San Francisco* (12), *Leave It To Henry* (12), *The Girl from Jones Beach* (12), *The Great Lover* (12), *Masked Raiders* (12), *Father Is a Bachelor* (13), *Father Makes Good* (13), *The Next Voice You Hear* (13), *Two Weeks with Love* (13), *Father's Wild Game* (13), *The Painted Hills* (14), and *Father Takes the Air* (14).

Gary enjoyed swimming, horseback riding, football, and baseball. He loved acting and his main ambition was to one day become a cowboy star. His education was acquired at the Mormon Tabernacle School and the Hollywood Professional Children's School.

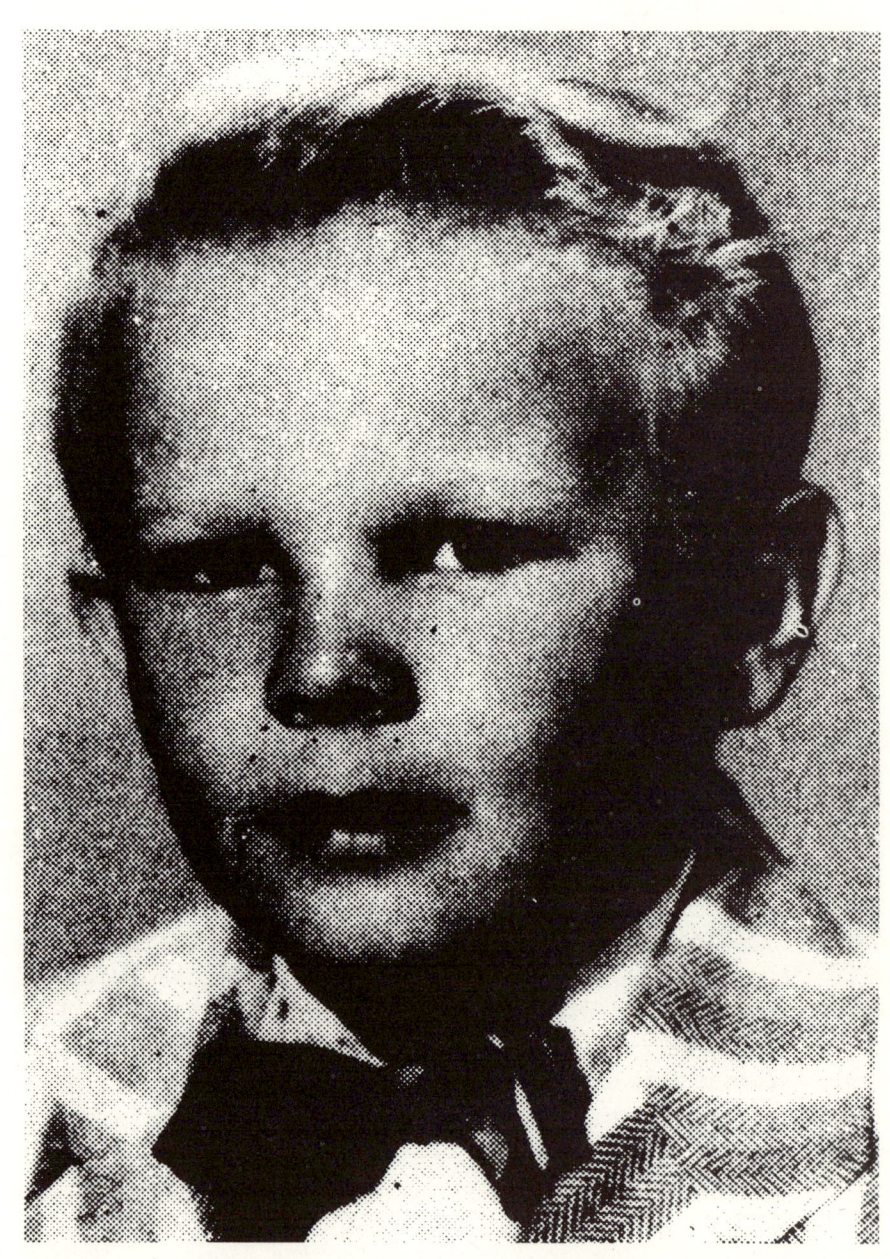

Fighting Back
(20th Century-Fox, 1948)

A parolee living an honest life in a small town is unjustly accused of stealing a valuable bracelet. Paul Langton starred as the ex-con, while Jean Rogers and Gary Gray were seen as his wife and son.

Rachel and the Stranger
(RKO Radio, 1948)

This adventure film about Ohio pioneers starred William Holden as a lonely farmer and Gary Gray as his motherless son.

The Night Wind
(20th Century-Fox, 1948)

Gary starred as a youngster who befriends an Army German shepherd dog believed to be the killer of two hunters.

The Night Wind
(20th Century-Fox, 1948)

In this feature Gary appeared opposite Charles Russell and Virginia Christine.

The Next Voice You Hear
(Metro-Goldwyn-Mayer, 1950)

This Dore Schary production narrates the story of a family who hear the voice of God over the radio. James Whitmore and Nancy Davis portrayed Mr. and Mrs. Smith, while Gary was seen as their son, Johnny.

DARLA HOOD

BORN: November 8, 1931. PLACE OF BIRTH: Leedey, Oklahoma. HAIR: Dark brown. EYES: Dark brown.

Darla Hood, the "little sweetheart" of *Our Gang,* was introduced to the professional arts at the age of three when she enrolled in an Oklahoma City talent school, which was run by a Miss Kathryn Duffy. When it became obvious that Darla had an exceptional aptitude for music, Miss Duffy obtained a few nightclub bookings for her in Chicago and New York. One evening while she dined at the Hotel Edison in Times Square, Darla was invited by the orchestra leader to take over the band. She accepted the request and the audience loved her. Joseph Rivkin, a talent scout for the Hal Roach Studios, tested the youngster in New York and signed her to a nine-year contract.

Between 1935 and 1941 Darla Hood made forty-eight *Our Gang* appearances. She debuted in an all-star revue entitled *Our Gang Follies of 1936* (4) and this led to some topflight performances in *Hearts Are Trumps* (5), *Mail and Female* (5), *Men In Fright* (6), and *Football Romeo* (6). Her final role came late in 1941 in an episode called *Wedding Worries* (10). Darla's feature film assignments were: *The Bohemian Girl* (4), *Neighborhood House* (4), *Born To Sing* (10), *The Happy Land* (11).

Her schooling was acquired at MGM's famous Little Red Schoolhouse where such celebrities as Mickey Rooney and Judy Garland received their education. Prior to her fifth birthday, little Darla Hood was earning $750 a week.

As an adult performer, Darla made two pictures. The first came in 1957 and was entitled *Calypso Heat Wave;* the second was the

Vincent Price horror-thriller *The Bat*, released in 1959. On television Darla appeared as Ken Murray's leading lady during the early fifties.

Our Gang Follies of 1936
(Roach-MGM, 1935)

Spanky McFarland and Darla Hood were two of the featured players in this short about the "Gang's" efforts in staging a revue.

The Bohemian Girl
(Metro-Goldwyn-Mayer, 1936)

Darla portrayed a little princess who is raised by two fun-loving gypsies. Stan Laurel and Oliver Hardy (in picture) are seen as the Romany rogues.

Our Gang Comedy
(Roach-MGM, 1937)

Members of the "Gang" seen in their clubhouse include Spanky McFarland, Buckwheat Thomas, Porky Lee, Alfalfa Switzer, and Darla Hood.

Our Gang Follies of 1938
(Roach-MGM, 1937)

Darla Hood is pictured here with Porky Lee in a scene from one of the "Gang's" musical shows.

The Happy Land
(20th Century-Fox, 1943)

This film was about an Iowa family and starred Richard Crane as a young man who is killed in battle and Ann Rutherford as his sweetheart. Darla Hood was seen in a flashback portraying Miss Rutherford at the age of twelve.

RA HOULD

BORN: January 21, 1924. PLACE OF BIRTH: Dunedin, New Zealand. HAIR: Brown. EYES: Blue.

When he was four years old, Ra Hould portrayed an elf in *Sleeping Beauty,* an operetta at the Princess Theatre in Dunedin, New Zealand. Dame Sybil Thorndike, the celebrated English actress, visited Dunedin in 1933 and was deeply impressed by the boy's performance in a play whereby he enacted the role of one of her children.

In 1934 the English colony's first talking picture was produced and Ra was chosen to handle the leading child's part. In order to further develop Ra's acting talents, his parents decided to move to England, but Dame Sybil advised them to try Hollywood instead.

Upon his arrival in Hollywood early in 1936, Ra was immediately assigned a part in the United Artists film *The Beloved Enemy* (12). Then came roles in *A Doctor's Diary* (12), *Dangerous Holiday* (13), and *Boots and Saddles* (13). For his fifth film, *Thoroughbreds Don't Cry* (13), Ra changed his name to Ronald Sinclair. His final film as a youngster was in MGM's *A Christmas Carol* (14).

Ra enjoyed a variety of activities. His hobbies were making model airplanes and reading detective magazines, while his favorite sports were swimming, horseback riding, and skating. He was especially fond of music and had spent five years studying the piano.

Beloved Enemy
(United Artists, 1936)

This drama about the Irish Rebellion of 1921 starred Ra Hould, Merle Oberon, and Brian Aherne.

A Doctor's Diary
(Paramount, 1937)

In this Charles Vidor release, Ra Hould portrays a musical whiz kid named Michael Fielding, who loses the use of an arm through a doctor's negligence.

Dangerous Holiday
(Republic, 1937)

Ra Hould appeared in a starring role as Ronnie Kimball, a violin prodigy who runs away from home. In his wanderings the boy stumbles into a gangsters' hideout and is instrumental in their capture.

Thoroughbreds Don't Cry
(Metro-Goldwyn-Mayer, 1937)

This film concerns an Englishman (C. Aubrey Smith) and his grandson (Ra Hould) who travel to America with a champion mare, hoping that the animal will win them a large stake.

Thoroughbreds Don't Cry
(Metro-Goldwyn-Mayer, 1937)

In this racetrack drama, Ra Hould starred opposite Mickey Rooney and Judy Garland.

CLAUDE JARMAN, JR.

BORN: September 27, 1934. PLACE OF BIRTH: Nashville, Tennessee. HAIR: Blond. EYES: Blue.

An MGM director named Clarence Brown signed Claude Jarman, Jr., for a role in *The Yearling* shortly after he spotted the boy in a fifth grade classroom at Nashville's Eakin School. It was the spring of 1946 and Brown was touring the Southern States in a determined effort to locate a youngster who could fit naturally into the role of Jody, the film's main character. Brown visited the Eakin School and was escorted by the principal to the fifth grade classes. Upon entering the first room he saw the boy standing at the blackboard. Claude looked perfect for the role of Jody with his long blond hair and gangly appearance. Accompanied by his father, Claude soon found himself Hollywood bound. A few screen tests convinced everyone of his potential and led to the signing of a seven-year contract.

In addition to *The Yearling*, which he made at the age of eleven, Claude had parts in these films: *High Barbaree* (12), *The Sun Comes Up* (14), *Roughshod* (14), *Intruder In the Dust* (14).

Claude was honored many times for his acting talents. He won *Film Daily*'s Critics Award for *The Yearling*, was voted one of the top five juvenile actors for 1946, was chosen by *Film Daily* as one of the top five "finds" of 1946, and was picked as a "star of tomorrow" in the *Motion Picture Herald-Fame* poll for 1947. All of the above were bestowed upon the boy despite the fact that he had never received any formal acting lessons.

His education was acquired at the MGM Studio School and he enjoyed leisure activities of football, baseball, and the Cub Scouts.

Claude Jarman had a number of important parts in movies from the age of fifteen until the age of seventeen. He was then out of films for three years, but returned in 1956 for a Walt Disney feature, *The Great Locomotive Chase*. Today, Claude Jarman is a successful public relations executive in San Francisco.

The Yearling
(Metro-Goldwyn-Mayer, 1947)

Clarence Brown directed this picture of a farm boy named Jody and his love for a pet fawn.

The Yearling
(Metro-Goldwyn-Mayer, 1947)

In this scene Jody is out camping with his best friend, Fodderwing, (Donn Gift), a young crippled boy.

High Barbaree
(Metro-Goldwyn-Mayer, 1947)

An Air Force pilot, while adrift in the Pacific, relives his past via flashbacks. Van Johnson was seen as the downed flyer and Claude Jarman, Jr., portrayed the character as a young boy. Thomas Mitchell (in picture) appeared as Captain Thad, a spinner of tall tales about a mythical island and the old G-note road (a mythical road on the mythical island of High Barbaree).

The Sun Comes Up
(Metro-Goldwyn-Mayer, 1949)

Claude appeared in this film as a shy orphan boy who is adopted by a widowed concert singer (Jeanette MacDonald) and her collie dog (Lassie). Lloyd Nolan also appeared.

Roughshod
(RKO Radio, 1949)

Robert Sterling had the lead role in this western film as a dude cowboy, while Claude played his range-hardened kid brother. Gloria Grahame also starred.

GLORIA JEAN

BORN: April 14, 1928. PLACE OF BIRTH: Buffalo, New York. HAIR: Reddish brown. EYES: Blue.

Gloria Jean was born in Buffalo, New York, but she moved with her family to Scranton, Pennsylvania, at the age of six months. Her professional career commenced by singing a little tune called "When I Take My Sugar To Tea" on a Scranton radio network at the age of three. In December of 1938 a group of Scranton citizens sent Gloria to New York for a singing audition. There she stayed and studied voice, made a number of appearances with the Colonial Opera Company, and became the youngest member of an operatic troupe in the country.

Joe Pasternak, a producer for Universal Pictures, brought Gloria Jean into motion pictures. In the spring of 1939, Pasternak was thinking of developing a young aspirant who could follow in Deanna Durbin's footsteps as the "queen of child virtuosos." Through one of his scouts, the producer was informed of the young singer and he interviewed her in New York. A term contract soon followed.

Her film credits are: *The Under-Pup* (11), *If I Had My Way* (11), *A Little Bit of Heaven* (12), *Never Give a Sucker An Even Break* (13), *What's Cookin'?* (13).

Upon the release of *Under-Pup*, Gloria was crowned "Queen of Anthracite" by Fred Huester, mayor of the coal-mining town of Scranton, Pennsylvania. During the eighteen months that preceded the signing of her Universal contract, Gloria Jean earned $10,000. In connection with showings of *A Little Bit of Heaven*, the youngster left Hollywood and embarked on a two-month personal appearance tour that covered over a dozen cities in the East and Midwest.

In her spare moments Gloria enjoyed horseback riding and swimming. She also played the piano. Education was via private tutor.

A very popular and extremely active performer throughout the forties, Gloria Jean began to lose her fan appeal with the dawning of a new decade and, in fact, she made only two more films—*Air Strike* in 1955 and *The Ladies Man* in 1961. Eleven years ago the former singer was employed as a hostess in the Tahitian Restaurant in Studio City. Later she became a receptionist for a cosmetics firm, and is now interested in making a comeback in show business as a country-western singer.

The Under-Pup
(Universal, 1939)

Gloria played a slum child who wins a trip to an exclusive girl's summer camp. There she finds difficulty adjusting and only one girl, Janet Cooper, becomes her friend. In this scene Gloria sings a melody for Janet (Virginia Weidler).

If I Had My Way
(Universal, 1940)

Gloria Jean was a nightclub performer in this film starring Bing Crosby.

A Little Bit of Heaven
(Universal, 1940)

In this film Gloria Jean was cast in the role of a young girl who becomes a hit radio performer.

Never Give a Sucker an Even Break
(Universal, 1941)

Playing the niece of W. C. Fields, Gloria Jean sings a few semiclassical numbers in this slapstick comedy.

What's Cookin'?
(Universal, 1942)

Gloria Jean starred with the Andrew Sisters, Leo Carrillo, and Franklin Pangborn (in picture) in this jive musical, which featured the sound of the Woody Herman Orchestra.

DICKIE JONES

BORN: February 25, 1927. PLACE OF BIRTH: Snyder, Texas. HAIR: Dark brown.

Unlike most child performers, Dickie Jones began his professional career in a spot far removed from the lavish sets of a Hollywood film studio. Known as the "little cowboy," Dickie was entertaining audiences at rodeos where, at the age of five, he would give riding and roping exhibitions. Hoot Gibson, popular Western filmstar, was one of many who viewed the youngster's act. Gibson hired the boy to perform with his traveling circus and billed him as the "youngest trick rider and roper in the world." Dickie starred with the circus for a year touring the United States and Canada, and then made his motion picture debut in *Wonder Bar* in early 1934.

Dickie appeared in *Little Men* (7), *The Hawk* (8), *Westward Ho!* (8), *Moonlight On the Prairie* (8), *Daniel Boone* (9), *The Black Legion* (9), *Stella Dallas* (10), *Blake of Scotland Yard* (10), *Renfrew of the Royal Mounted* (10), *Hollywood Roundup* (10), *Love Is On the Air* (10), *The Kid Comes Back* (10), *Border Wolves* (10), *Flying Fists* (10), *The Devil's Party* (11), *The Great Adventures of Wild Bill Hickok* (11), *A Man To Remember* (11), *The Frontiersman* (11), *Woman Doctor* (11), *Sergeant Madden* (11), *I Am Not Afraid* (12), *Sky Patrol* (12), *The Man Who Dared* (12), *Destry Rides Again* (12), *Virginia City* (12), *Maryland* (13), *Brigham Young—Frontiersman* (13), *The Howards of Virginia* (13), *Adventure In Washington* (14), and *The Vanishing Virginian* (14).

In addition to his many film roles, Dickie Jones was cast in numerous short features. He was seen in the Edgar Kennedy comedy *Gasoloons* (8), in 1936, and he had parts in four *Our Gang* comedies: *Our Gang Follies of 1936* (8), *Pinch Singer* (8), *Pigskin Palooka* (10), *Our Gang Follies of 1938* (10). Probably his most noteworthy assignment came at the age of thirteen when he provided the voice of Pinocchio for the Walt Disney cartoon. Then, at the age of fourteen, he was heard from coast-to-coast in the leading role of the successful radio series "Henry Aldrich."

In 1951 Dick Jones was featured with Jock Mahoney in television's "Range Rider" series. Following the show's cancellation in 1954, Dick became the star of a series entitled "Buffalo Bill, Jr." Since 1960, however, he has made only an occasional guest appearance on television.

The Black Legion
(Warner Brothers, 1936)

Humphrey Bogart starred as a factory worker who joined a hooded organization called the Black Legion. Dickie played his son, Buddy.

The Kid Comes Back
(Warner Brothers, 1938)

In this prize-fight melodrama, Wayne Morris portrayed a scrappy kid from Texas, while Dickie played his newsboy pal, Bobby Doyle.

Destry Rides Again
(Universal, 1939)

Dickie had a small role as a rancher's son in this Pasternak western starring James Stewart.

Virginia City
(Warner Brothers, 1940)

Dickie appeared in this Civil War drama opposite Errol Flynn and Randolph Scott.

Brigham Young—Frontiersman
(20th Century-Fox, 1940)

Dickie appeared in a supporting role as the son of a Mormon zealot (Tyrone Power). Linda Darnell also starred.

TERRY KILBURN

BORN: November 25, 1926. PLACE OF BIRTH: London, England. HAIR: Brown. EYES: Gray green.

Though there had never been any performers in the Kilburn family, Terry was encouraged in his acting pursuits. He presented his first performances at theaters and children's concerts giving impersonations of well-known English actors.

Because of the British laws governing the appearance of screen children, Terry was limited in the amount of experience he could acquire. Therefore, his parents brought him to the 'States with the aid of a prominent Los Angeles attorney named Roger Marchetti. Through Marchetti, Terry became acquainted with the popular radio comedian Eddie Cantor. Accepting a part on Cantor's radio program, Terry gave a recitation about a little boy's unsuccessful attempts in redeeming his dog from the pound. Casting officials from MGM heard the broadcast and offered the boy a screen test for their upcoming film, *Lord Jeff*. Terry won the part and his movie career was launched.

Following *Lord Jeff* (11), he had assignments in *A Christmas Carol* (11), *Sweethearts* (11), *Goodbye, Mr. Chips* (12), *Andy Hardy Gets Spring Fever* (12), *They Shall Have Music* (12), *The Adventures of Sherlock Holmes* (12), *Swiss Family Robinson* (13), and *Mercy Island* (14).

Terry was educated by private tutors. He enjoyed the sports of swimming and roller skating, while his favorite hobby was sketching. He loved the motion-picture profession and hoped to one day become a costume designer.

A Christmas Carol
(Metro-Goldwyn-Mayer, 1938)

Charles Dickens's story of an antisocial old man was brought to the screen with Terry Kilburn (center) in the role of Tiny Tim, the crippled son of a timid clerk, and with Reginald Owen in the lead role of Ebenezer Scrooge.

Sweethearts
(Metro-Goldwyn-Mayer, 1938)

Jeanette MacDonald and Nelson Eddy appeared as the lead players in this movie about two aging Broadway stars. Terry was seen as their son.

Goodbye, Mr. Chips
(Metro-Goldwyn-Mayer, 1939)

This film, adapted from the James Hilton novel, starred Robert Donat and Greer Garson. Terry Kilburn had the role of Peter Colley, a mischievous young lad attending the Brookfield School.

Andy Hardy Gets Spring Fever
(Metro-Goldwyn-Mayer, 1939)

Terry co-starred as "Stickin' Plaster" in this Andy Hardy comedy, which finds the hero (Mickey Rooney) involved in a one-sided romance with his schoolteacher.

Swiss Family Robinson
(RKO Radio, 1940)

Ernest Robinson (Terry) and his family are shipwrecked on an island en route to Australia. Thomas Mitchell starred as the father.

MARK LESTER

BORN: July 11, 1958. PLACE OF BIRTH: Oxford, England. HAIR: Blond.

Mark was born in Oxford, England, but moved with his family to Richmond, near London, when he was just an infant. Britain's best-loved child performer first appeared before the cameras doing television commercials at the age of two and a half. Michael Lester, Mark's father, was producing television commercials for the British networks in 1960 and, when he learned that a small boy was needed for a role, he immediately suggested his son. Mark tested for the part, and won it.

In 1961 Mark began his film career when casting officials from the Pinewood Studios became attracted to his commercial work. He was used for a brief scene in *Sanctuary*. During the next five years, Mark performed in a host of motion pictures, but his parts were mainly secondary. Then, in 1967, the boy drew prestigious acclaim with his portrayal of Jiminy in *Our Mother's House*. When auditions for *Oliver* began a year later, the youngster found himself in competition with 250 applicants. However, through his experience in *House* and with a superb recommendation from its director, Jack Clayton, Mark was chosen for the title role.

Mark performed in these films: *Spaceflight IC-1* (7), *Fahrenheit 451* (8), *Our Mother's House* (9), *Oliver* (10), *Run Wild, Run Free* (10), *Sudden Terror* (12), *Melody* (12), *Black Beauty* (12), *Who Slew Auntie Roo?* (13), *What the Peeper Saw* (14). On American television he guest starred in "Then Came Bronson" (10), "The Ghost and Mrs. Muir" (11), "The Wonderful World of Disney" (11).

Mark has been recognized for his acting abilities on a number of occasions. He won the *Film Daily* Critics Award in 1967, gave one of the top five juvenile acting performances for that year in *Our Mother's House,* and received the award again the following year for *Oliver*. Mark also won an award at the Moscow Art Festival for his work in *Oliver*.

Mark's education was acquired at the Corona Stage School in London and by private tutors. He lists rugby as his favorite pastime.

Nowadays, Mark Lester is a very busy youngster, making personal appearance tours throughout the United States, France, Japan, China, and Germany. He has a number of films up for release such as *Redneck* and *Scalawag* in which he is to perform opposite Telly Savalas and Kirk Douglas, respectively.

Our Mother's House
(Metro-Goldwyn-Mayer, 1967)

Mark's first starring role had him portraying a little boy named Jiminee, who is afflicted with the stutters. He is shown here with Dirk Bogarde.

Oliver
(Columbia Pictures, 1968)

During mealtime at a nineteenth-century English orphanage, young Oliver Twist asks for a second helping of gruel. In this scene the workhouse proprietor escorts the young lad out of the dining area.

Oliver
(Columbia Pictures, 1968)

Here Mark is shown with Ron Moody, who appeared in the film as Fagin. Mark sang "Where Is Love?"

Run Wild, Run Free
(Columbia Pictures, 1969)

In this feature Mark played the part of a ten-year-old boy who befriends a white stallion that runs wild on the moors surrounding his home. Here he is with a neighbor girl, Diana, and her pet kestrel.

Black Beauty
(Paramount, 1971)

Mark had a brief but endearing role in the fourth filming of the Anna Sewell novel. He handled the part of an English farm boy named Joe Evans, who was given a black foal as a gift. Both lead a happy life until pending bankruptcy forced Joe's father to sell the animal.

JERRY MATHERS (THE BEAVER)

BORN: June 2, 1948. PLACE OF BIRTH: Sioux City, Iowa. HAIR: Brown. EYES: Blue.

A department-store saleslady in Sioux City, Iowa, started Jerry Mathers on a professional career. The salesgirl felt Jerry had definite possibilities as a model and she urged the lad's mother to look into the matter. Mrs. Mathers brought her year-old son to the store's advertising manager who, in turn, hired the boy to model various baby ensembles for the city newspapers. A portrait photographer noticed one of the advertisements and the youngster was soon posing for magazines.

Early in 1953 Jerry was introduced to a theatrical agent. Various interviews led to a number of small assignments on television, but nothing more. At this time Jerry's modeling career took on a new look when he was joined by his sister, Suzie. They modeled together for a couple of years, then were noticed by talent scouts from RKO Radio Pictures and assigned parts in *This Is My Love*.

This Is My Love (6) was followed by solo performances in *The Trouble With Harry* (7), *That Certain Feeling* (7), *Bigger Than Life* (8), and *Shadow On the Window* (8). On television Jerry had the title role in the ABC series "Leave It To Beaver" (9-14).

He was awarded the Milky Way Gold Star Award for 1959 as one of the nation's twelve most talented child performers and the state of Oregon (Beaver State) made him an honorary citizen following the presentation. Jerry kept himself occupied by playing baseball and collecting toy soldiers.

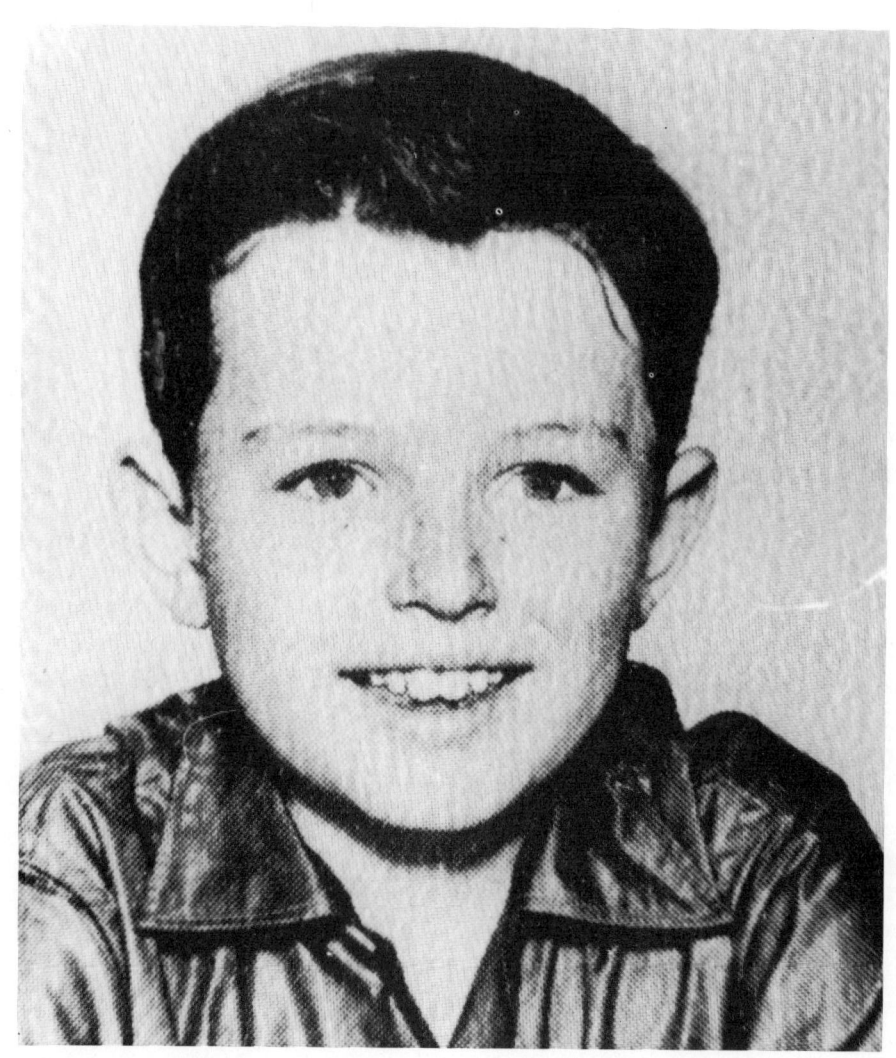

This Is My Love
(RKO Radio, 1954)

Jerry co-stars with his younger sister in this soap opera opposite lead players Linda Darnell and Dan Duryea.

The Trouble With Harry
(Paramount, 1956)

Jerry appeared with Shirley MacLaine and John Forsythe in this murder-melodrama produced and directed by Alfred Hitchcock.

That Certain Feeling
(Paramount, 1956)

Bob Hope had the starring role in this comedy of a practicing cartoonist and his unnerving relationship with a celebrated comic-strip artist (George Sanders). Jerry had the role of a small, adopted boy.

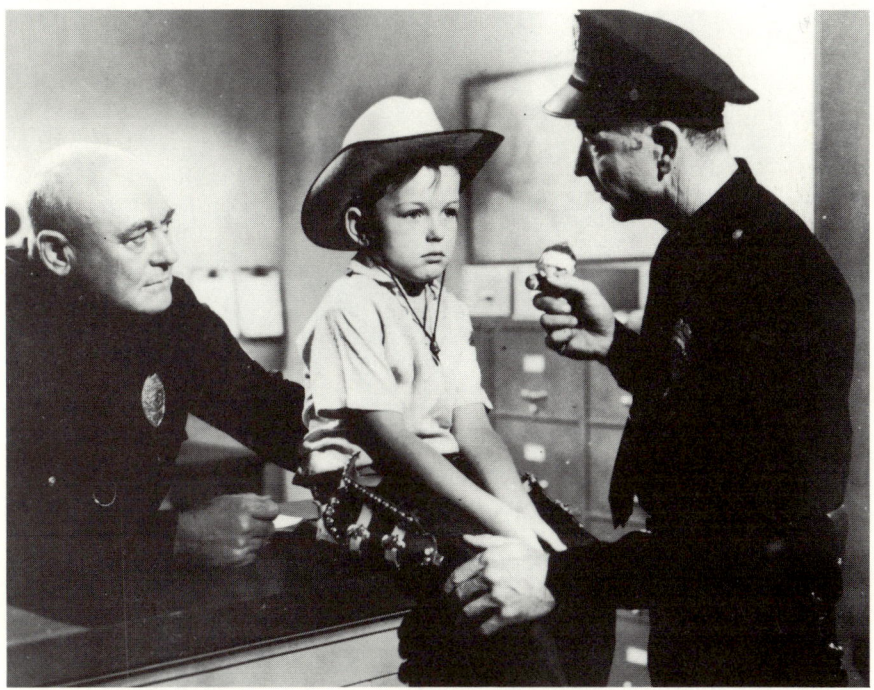

The Shadow on the Window
(Columbia Pictures, 1957)

In this thriller Jerry portrayed a shock-muted boy who witnesses a murder, and the kidnapping of his mother by three delinquents.

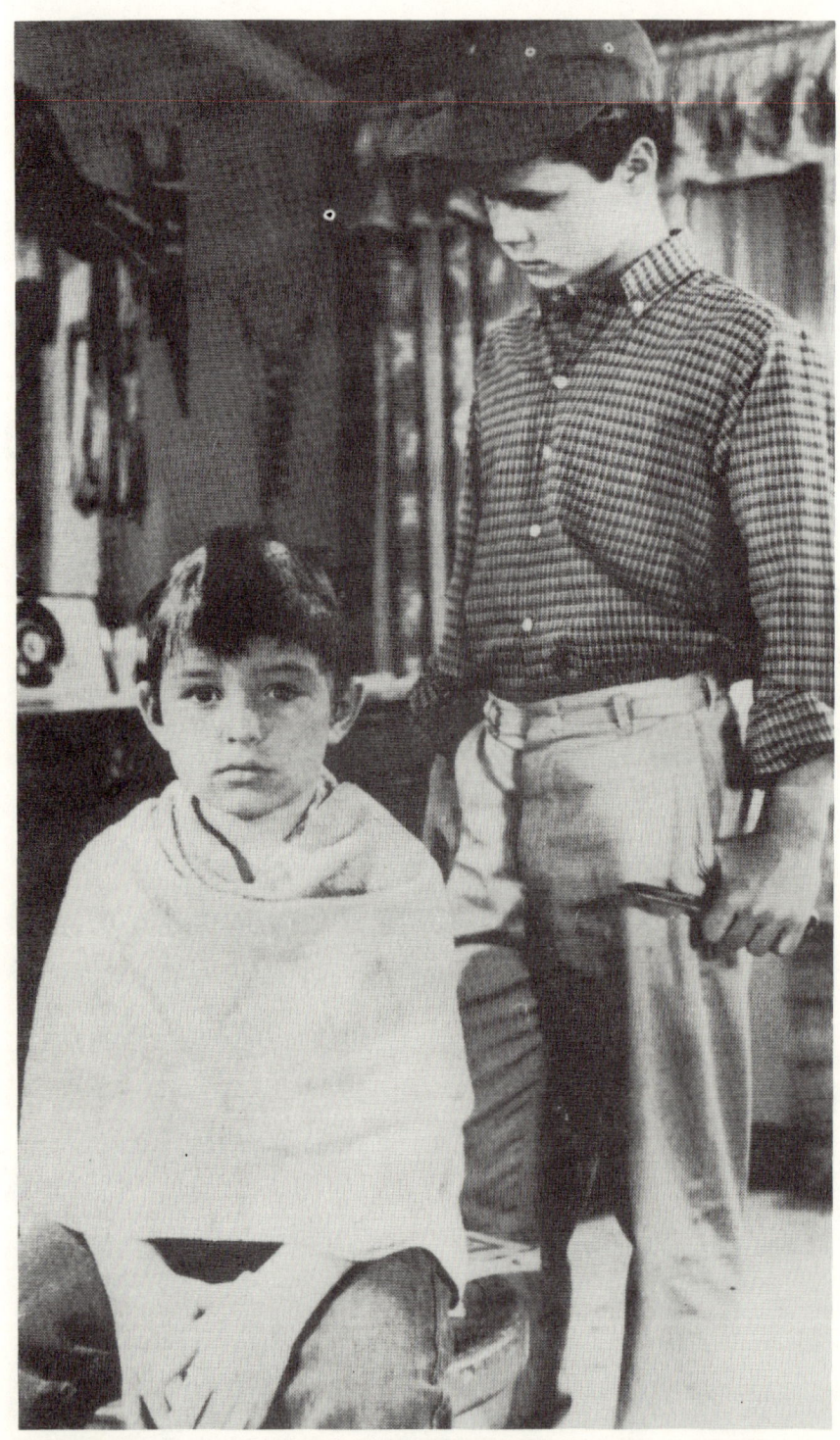

"Leave It To Beaver"
(ABC TV, 1957)

Beaver (Jerry Mathers) loses the money that his father has given him for a haircut, so his brother, Wally, decides to do the job. Tony Dow was seen as Beaver's older brother.

THE MAUCH TWINS

BORN: July 6, 1924. PLACE OF BIRTH: Peoria, Illinois. HAIR: Dark brown. EYES: Blue.

Billy and Bobby Mauch were born entertainers. When the twins were four years old, they accompanied their mother in singing bedtime songs. Two years later the twins were appearing on the radio and at Elks' assemblies in Peoria. When the boys were eight years old, they moved to New York. The two were in demand for radio performances almost immediately and were on such programs as the "Beauty Box Review," "Lucky Strike," "Show Boat," "March of Time," and many others.

A friend of the family contacted Mrs. Mauch in the fall of 1935 informing her that a movie company sought a young boy to perform in *Anthony Adverse*. Two weeks after they visited the Warner Brother's casting office, Billy and Bobby had signed their movie contracts. In Hollywood, after thorough examination of the screen tests, director Mervyn Leroy chose Billy for the role and made Bobby his stand-in. Their salary a year later stood at $350 a week.

Following *Anthony Adverse* (11), Billy made two solo performances in *The White Angel* (11) and *Penrod and Sam* (12). He then joined his brother for the title role in *The Prince and the Pauper* (12), and later they made *Penrod and His Twin Brother* (13) and *Penrod's Double Trouble* (13).

They acquired their education at the Professional Children's School in New York and by private tutors in Hollywood. Pastimes were swimming, football, and pingpong. Billy's hobby was photography, but both boys collected stamps. Outside of acting, they could sing, dance, and play the piano.

Billy Mauch

Bobby Mauch

Anthony Adverse
(Warner Brothers, 1936)

Billy had the role of Anthony Adverse, a foundling in a convent, who is apprenticed at the age of ten to a merchant named John Bonnyfeather. Billy is pictured with Edmund Gwenn, who played Bonnyfeather.

Penrod and Sam
(Warner Brothers, 1937)

In this third filming of the Booth Tarkington novel, Penrod and Sam are junior G-men who manage to capture three notorious killers. Billy played Penrod and Harry Watson appeared as Sam.

The Prince and the Pauper
(Warner Brothers, 1937)

In this adaptation of the Mark Twain novel, Billy Mauch portrayed a beggar named Tom Canty who trades in his rags for the robes of Prince Edward, his look-alike. Bobby Mauch had the role of the young prince.

The Prince and the Pauper
(Warner Brothers, 1937)

Young Prince Edward (Bobby Mauch) accepts the king's crown about to be administered to him by the Archbishop (Halliwell Hobbes).

Penrod and His Twin Brother
(Warner Brothers, 1938)

In this film Billy appeared in the name role, while Bobby played a young roughneck. Together they start a game of junior G-men, which ultimately leads in their being captured by gangsters.

JACKIE MORAN

BORN: January 26, 1925. PLACE OF BIRTH: Chicago, Illinois. HAIR: Light brown. EYES: Blue.

At the age of eight, Jackie Moran was singing with a choir in his hometown. Jackie's mother, who was once a concert singer, decided that a professional career could be in the offering for her son and arranged for him to become a model. Commercial photography work followed in which he posed for pictures to be used in automobile, soft drink, and clothes advertisements.

While attending the play *The Church Mouse* in Chicago in 1935, Jackie went backstage to obtain the star's (Mary Pickford) autograph. Miss Pickford liked the boy; she was quite amused by his mannerisms and urged his mother to bring him to Hollywood. Jackie left for the West Coast, where he won a movie role in Columbia's *And So They Were Married* (11).

Following this performance, Jackie appeared in *Valiant Is the Word for Carrie* (11), *Outcast* (11), *Michael O'Halloran* (12), *The Adventures of Tom Sawyer* (12), *Mad About Music* (13), *Arson Gang Busters* (13), *Mother Carey's Chickens* (13), *Barefoot Boy* (13), *Buck Rogers* (14), *The Spirit of Culver* (14), *Everybody's Hobby* (14), and *Meet Dr. Christian* (14).

Jackie loved a good game of baseball. He was educated at the Professional Children's School in Hollywood.

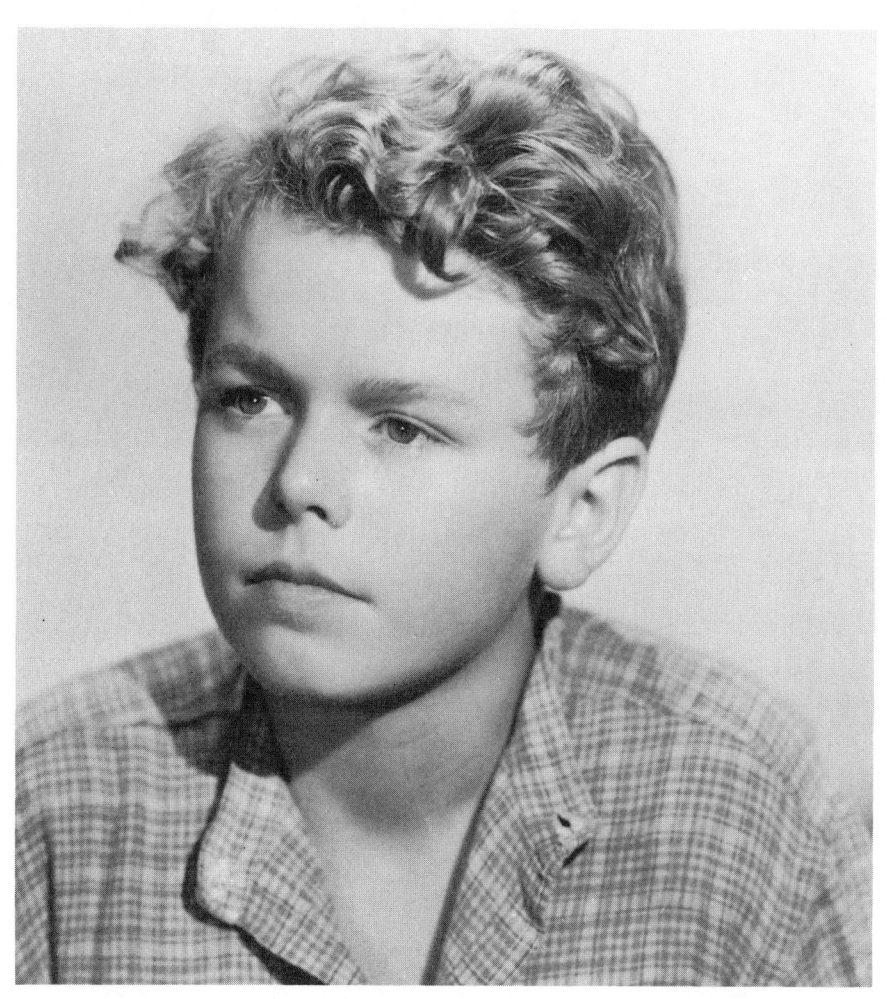

Valiant Is the Word for Carrie
(Paramount, 1936)

In this film Jackie portrayed a youngster who is adopted by a woman of ill repute. The woman (Gladys George) falls in love with the boy and his little sister, Lady, and takes them to New York to build a new life.

Michael O'Halloran
(Republic, 1937)

Jackie had a starring role opposite Warren Hull and Sidney Blackmer.

The Adventures of Tom Sawyer
(United Artists, 1938)

In this third filming of the classic Mark Twain novel, Jackie Moran is cast as Huckleberry Finn. Here he is seen with Victor Jory who portrayed Injun Joe.

Mother Carey's Chickens
(RKO Radio, 1938)

A widowed mother and her five children, about to be dispossessed from their New England home, scare off possible buyers by declaring the house to be haunted. Fay Bainter played the title role, while Jackie played one of her "chickens."

Buck Rogers
(Universal, 1939)

Buck Rogers (Buster Crabbe) and Buddy Wade (Jackie Moran) assist a scientist in his efforts to conquer a horde of gangsters led by a notorious killer. In this scene Buck, Buddy, and Wilma, the scientist's lovely daughter (Constance Moore), head for Saturn to enlist the aid of the Saturnians.

DANNY MUMMERT

BORN: February 20, 1934. PLACE OF BIRTH: Dallas, Texas. HAIR: Brown. EYES: Brown.

At the age of two Danny Mummert was featured in a *Dallas News* write-up. The article spoke of the child's amazing powers of memorization at the 1936 Texas Centennial Fair where he mystified patrons by reciting the names of the United States Presidents and the state capitals. A year later, Mrs. Mummert brought her son to Hollywood, but casting officials were not overly impressed by the youngster's precocity. After this unsuccessful venture, Danny enrolled in the Meglin School for Kiddies in an effort to develop his acting talents.

Danny was a pupil of the Meglin School for almost a year. Finally he received a call to be interviewed. Columbia Pictures was busy screening children for roles in a movie based upon the comic strip *Blondie*. The studio originally intended casting Danny as Blondie's son, but when this part was handed to Larry Simms at the last moment, Danny was used as the next-door neighbor's boy, Alvin.

On the screen Danny performed in *Blondie* (4), *Blondie Meets the Boss* (5), *Blondie Takes a Vacation* (5), *Blondie Brings Up Baby* (5), *Blondie On a Budget* (6), *Blondie Has Servant Trouble* (6), *Blondie Plays Cupid* (6), *Blondie Goes Latin* (6), *Blondie In Society* (7), *Thunder Over the Prairie* (7), *The Stork Pays Off* (7), *Blondie Goes To College* (7), *Blondie's Blessed Event* (8), *Meet the Stewarts* (8), *Blondie for Victory* (8), *It's a Great Life* (9), *Footlight Glamour* (9), *Beautiful But Broke* (9), *Leave It To Blondie* (10), *Senorita From the West* (11), *Blondie Knows Best* (12), *Blondie's Big Moment* (12), *Blondie In the Dough* (13), *Blondie's Reward* (14), *Blondie's Secret* (14), and *Blondie's Big Deal* (14).

Thunder Over the Prairie
(Columbia Pictures, 1941)

In this western musical Danny Mummert performed alongside Charles Starrett. He is pictured here with Carl Shrum and his Rhythm Rangers.

The Stork Pays Off
(Columbia Pictures, 1941)

Danny Mummert, a Bowery brat attending a swank private school, appeared in a lead role opposite Maxie Rosenbloom.

Meet the Stewarts
(Columbia Pictures, 1942)

Danny co-starred in this comedy-feature about the budget problems of a newly wed couple. William Holden and Frances Dee portrayed the troubled newlyweds. Danny had the role of Miss Dee's little brother.

Leave It to Blondie
(Columbia Pictures, 1945)

Alvin (Danny Mummert) sings at the Bumstead breakfast table for Dagwood (Arthur Lake) and Alexander (Larry Simms).

Blondie Knows Best
(Columbia Pictures, 1946)

Abby Berlin took over the directorial reins for this Blondie episode in which both Danny Mummert and Larry Simms had starring roles opposite Penny Singleton.

DONALD O'CONNOR

BORN: August 28, 1925. PLACE OF BIRTH: Chicago, Illinois. HAIR: Light brown. EYES: Blue.

Donald O'Connor was born into a show-business family. His father John (Chuck) O'Connor was a onetime acrobat for the Ringling Brothers Circus, while his mother was a tightrope walker and bareback rider. Later, both parents took up the vaudeville circuit and with their seven children they became "The O'Connor Family Act." Donald had makeup on at the age of two months when his parents first carried him on stage at the conclusion of each performance. Donald joined the act as a performer at the age of one and his first assignment came in Columbus, Ohio, where he did a solo dance number called the "black bottom." At the age of three, he began tap dancing with the troupe and, a year later, made his singing debut with a little tune entitled "Keep Your Sunny Side Up."

While performing at the Biltmore Theater in Los Angeles during a 1938 charity benefit, Donald was noticed by a Paramount assistant director named Artie Jackson and signed to a one-year contract at $250 a week. Actually, Donald had made his motion picture debut a year earlier in the Warner Brother's production *Melody for Two* (11), but it was with Paramount that the boy made his mark in films.

His other screen credits are: *Sing, You Sinners* (12), *Sons of the Legion* (12), *Men With Wings* (13), *Tom Sawyer, Detective* (13), *Boy Trouble* (13), *Unmarried* (13), *Beau Geste* (13), *Death of a Champion* (13), *Million Dollar Legs* (13), *Night Work* (13), *On Your Toes* (14).

In addition to touring the vaudeville circuit with his family, Donald also performed with the vaudeville team "Sons O' Fun" in Syracuse, New York. He played all the top circuits of his day, which included the Keith-Orpheum, Bert Levy, and Joe Daniels' theaters.

During his vaudeville career, Donald received an education backstage. In Hollywood he attended the studio school at Paramount and the Professional Children's School.

Donald became a celebrity performer during the '50s. He starred in seven "Francis the Mule" pictures between 1949 and 1956, but gave his finest portrayals in films like: *Yes Sir, That's My Baby, Walking My Baby Back Home,* and *There's No Business Like Show Business.* Donald's last movie role came in 1965 when he made *That Funny Feeling.*

Sons of the Legion
(Paramount, 1938)

Donald played a young ruffian whose war veteran father was serving a lengthy prison term.

Boy Trouble
(Paramount, 1939)

Donald appeared as a homeless waif in this comedy film. Mary Boland and Charlie Ruggles played a small-town, childless couple who adopt Donald and a little orphan boy (Billy Lee).

Unmarried
(Paramount, 1939)

In this feature Donald starred alongside Buck Jones and Helen Twelvetrees.

Death of a Champion
(Paramount, 1939)

This film deals with two amateur sleuths who attempt to solve the mystifying death of a champion show dog. Donald starred with Lynne Overman.

Night Work
(Paramount, 1939)

Mary Boland and Charlie Ruggles join Donald as the principals of a comedy-feature in which Ruggles is the manager of a large apartment house.

DAWN O'DAY

BORN: April 17, 1918. PLACE OF BIRTH: New York City. HAIR: Red. EYES: Brown.

Dawn O'Day, born Dawn Eveleen Paris, started her professional career at the age of fourteen months by posing for a commercial artist. The child's reddish curly hair attracted the painter so he hired her to model a series of drawings on baby clothes. Dawn modeled until the summer of 1922 at which time she undertook a film career with a substantial part in *Moonshine Valley* (4). Shortly after completing the aforementioned picture, Dawn moved from New York to Hollywood, since the latter offered more opportunity for success.

Upon arrival in Hollywood, Mrs. O'Day contacted Paramount Pictures to obtain an interview for her daughter. Herbert Brenon, who directed Dawn in her first film, was in the process of making *The Spanish Dancer* and he required a moppet for a significant role. Dawn was handed the assignment as soon as Brenon heard of her availability.

Following *Spanish Dancer,* which she did at the age of five, Dawn appeared in *The Man Who Fights Alone* (6), *The Fast Set* (6), *Riders of the Purple Sage* (6), *The Callahans and the Murphys* (9), *Night Life* (9), *Mother Knows Best* (10), *Four Devils* (10), *Sins of the Fathers* (10), *City Girl* (11), *Gun Smoke* (12), *Rich Man's Folly* (13), *So Big* (13), and *Young America* (13).

Dawn received an education through private tutors and her free time was spent in taking dancing lessons at the Lawler's Dancing School.

In the latter part of 1934, Dawn O'Day began a new phase of

her career. Cast in the title role of *Anne of Green Gables,* Dawn changed her name and became Anne Shirley. Remembered today as one of Hollywood's most renowned performers, Annie Shirley was given leading parts in over twenty motion pictures. Some of her best known vehicles are: *Stella Dallas* (1937), *Saturday's Children* (1940), and *Anne of Windy Poplars* (1940). *Make Mine Laughs* was Anne's final movie. It was released by RKO Radio Pictures in August of 1949.

The Man Who Fights Alone
(Paramount, 1924)

In this William Farnum silent, Dawn O'Day portrayed the four-year-old daughter of a paralyzed civil engineer.

The Fast Set
(Paramount, 1924)

This picture about the misadventures of a young married couple starred Betty Compson (in picture) and Elliott Dexter, with Dawn O'Day appearing as their little daughter. The film was directed by William DeMille and adapted from the play *Spring Cleaning*.

Mother Knows Best
(20th Century-Fox, 1928)

Dawn was seen briefly in the opening scenes of this film portraying a little girl who is pushed into a stage career by an overbearing mother (Louise Dresser).

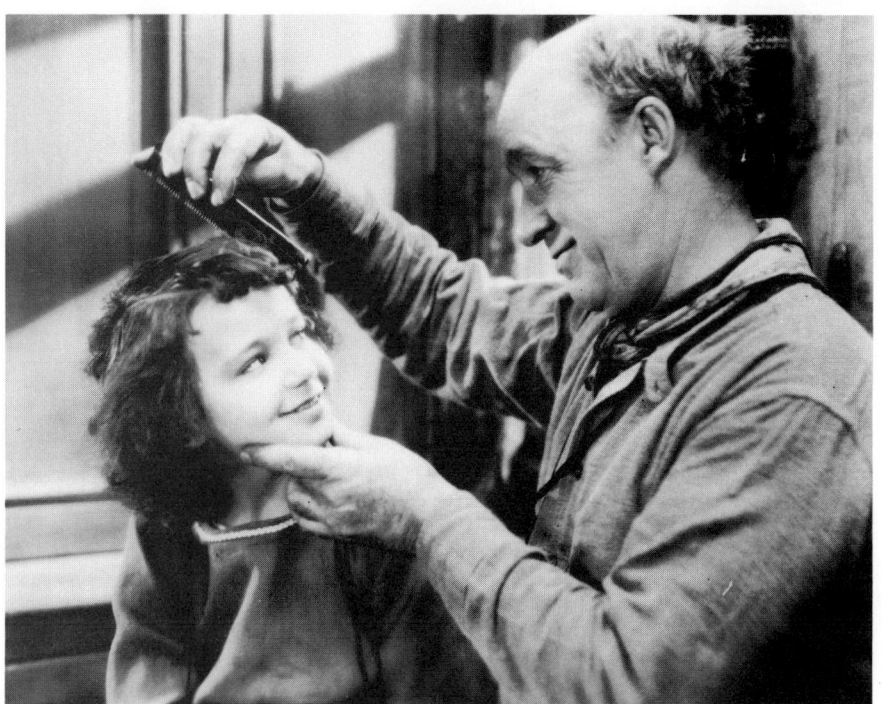

Four Devils
(20th Century-Fox, 1928)

In this tale of circus life Dawn portrayed a young acrobat.

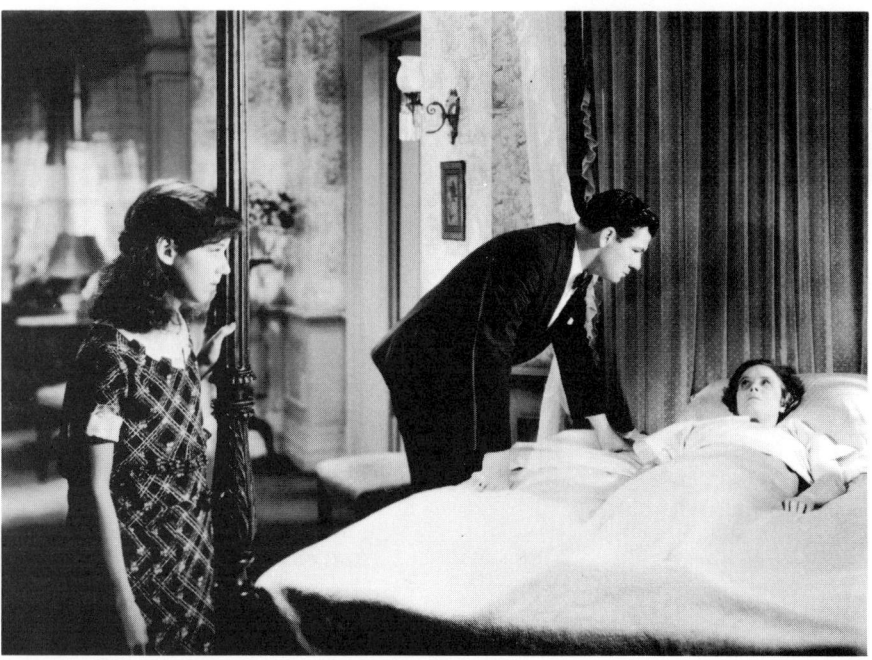

Rich Man's Folly
(Paramount, 1931)

Following her mother's death, a young girl named Anne is shunned by her father and sent away to boarding school. Dawn is cast as Anne, while George Bancroft played her father. The film is loosely adapted from Dickens's novel, *Dombey and Son*.

PATSY LEE PARSONS

BORN: June 9, 1931. PLACE OF BIRTH: Parkersburg, West Virginia. HAIR: Curly brown. EYES: Blue.

In early 1936, Patsy Lee Parsons traveled north to New York City for a brief visit. While she was there, a benefit show was staged at Madison Square Garden. Patsy Lee, who attended a dancing school in Parkersburg, decided to entertain for the charity and she performed a brief song-and-dance routine. Arthur Tracy, the street singer, appeared on the same program. The youngster's performance stuck in his mind and a few days later he introduced Patsy Lee to a talent scout named Lou Erwin. Erwin thought so highly of the little girl that he procured her a screen test in New York with RKO Radio Pictures. A year after her arrival in New York, Patsy Lee Parsons had become an actress with the release of RKO's *They Wanted To Marry* (5).

Her other film assignments were: *Meet Dr. Christian* (8), *Heroes of the Saddle* (8), *Melody for Three* (9), *The Affairs of Jimmy Valentine* (10), *Yankee Doodle Dandy* (10), and *Roughly Speaking* (13).

Meet Dr. Christian
(RKO Radio, 1939)

In this film Patsy Lee portrayed the daughter of the town mayor. Jackie Moran was also featured.

Melody for Three
(RKO Radio, 1941)

Patsy Lee co-starred with Irene Ryan in this musical-feature.

The Affairs of Jimmy Valentine
(Republic, 1942)

Patsy Lee was featured along with Dennis O'Keefe.

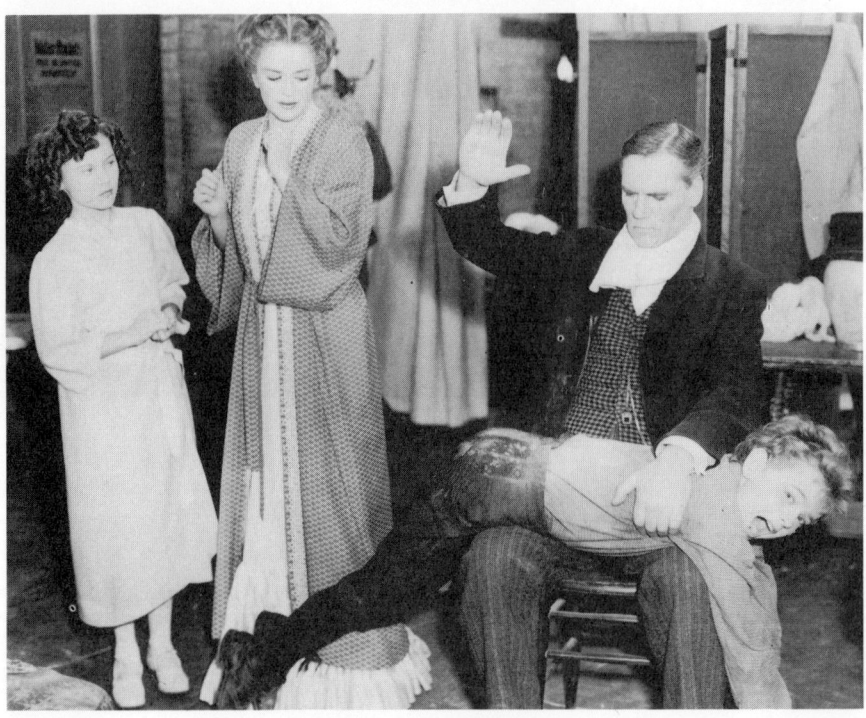

Yankee Doodle Dandy
(Warner Brothers, 1942)

This picture honoring the famous song-and-dance man George M. Cohan, starred James Cagney and Walter Huston. Patsy Lee had the part of Cohan's sister, Josie, as a young girl. Rosemary DeCamp played the mother and Douglas Croft played Cohan as a boy.

Roughly Speaking
(Warner Brothers, 1945)

This film traced the life of an American girl during the early part of the twentieth century. Rosalind Russell portrayed Louise Randall, daughter of a New England merchant, while Patsy Lee played one of her four children and Jack Oakie played the father. The picture was based on the biography of Louise Randall Pierson.

LUANA PATTEN

BORN: July 6, 1938. PLACE OF BIRTH: Long Beach, California. HAIR: Light brown. EYES: Big and blue.

Shortly after her third birthday, Luana Patten was hired by a commercial photographer to pose for a soap advertisement. It was the beginning of a highly prosperous modeling career, which in a two-year span saw her grace the pages of over 150 magazines throughout the country. Luana was a cover girl for nearly four years and in the process earned the title of "young America's sweetheart."

Luana began her film career in 1945 with a minor role in MGM's *Little Mr. Jim* (7). A year later she was interviewed by Walt Disney at the Burbank Studios and signed to a term contract. Disney starred her first in *Song of the South* (8), then gave her leading assignments in *Fun and Fancy Free* (9), *Melody Time* (9), and *So Dear To My Heart* (10).

Song of the South was the moppet's finest picture. She attended the film's world premiere showing in Los Angeles and then toured the South in a publicity campaign. *Film Daily* honored Luana by bestowing on her the Critics Award, and her performance was voted to be one of the five best by a juvenile actress.

In 1948 Luana's Disney contract expired and was not renewed. The child had found much success in films till then and could have continued to do so for many years to come. However, her parents decided it was best that she concentrate on her schooling and develop a more normal social life.

Luana returned to acting upon completion of her high school studies. Her first picture in a comeback effort was Universal's *Rock,*

Pretty Baby (1958). She followed this with appearances in *Home From the Hill* (1960), *A Thunder of Drums* (1961), and *Follow Me Boys* (1966).

Song of the South
(RKO Radio, 1946)

Walt Disney's live action-animated film starred Luana Patten as a poor, little girl named Ginny who found solace in Uncle Remus, a teller of animal fables. Luana is pictured with Bobby Driscoll, a lonely youngster who becomes her playmate.

Fun and Fancy Free
(RKO Radio, 1947)

In this Disney feature Luana starred with Edgar Bergen, Charlie McCarthy, and Mortimer Snerd. Also in the picture were Donald Duck, Mickey Mouse, and Jiminy Cricket.

Fun and Fancy Free
(RKO Radio, 1947)

In this Disney production Edgar Bergen tells Luana Patten the story of "Mickey and the Beanstalk," in which Mickey Mouse attempts to retrieve a magic, singing harp from the clutches of an evil giant.

So Dear to My Heart
(RKO Radio, 1948)

In this cartoon-and-live action Disney feature, Luana Patten starred alongside Bobby Driscoll. The film was based on the fable by Sterling North. Beulah Bondi and Edgar Buchanan (both in picture) were also featured.

So Dear to My Heart
(RKO Radio, 1948)

Luana, as Tildy, appeared as the charming companion and friend of a mischievous country boy.

BABY PEGGY

BORN: October 26, 1918. PLACE OF BIRTH: Merced, California. HAIR: Brown. EYES: Brown.

Julius Stern, director of Universal's *Century Comedies,* discovered Baby Peggy while he was visiting Yellowstone Park. The year was 1919. Peggy lived at Yellowstone where her father, Jack Montgomery, had accepted the duties of forest ranger.

Early in 1920 while on vacation in San Francisco, the family recalled Stern's invitation to visit him. Stern, who was then in the process of filming a comedy entitled *Playmates,* sought a little girl to perform opposite Brownie, one of filmdom's leading canine performers. Using her charm and grown-up personality, Peggy easily completed a screen test that the director arranged. She then was starred in six dog-and-baby comedies and over forty *Century Comedies.* Some of her most notable performances are in *Peggy, Behave* (3), *Carmen, Jr.* (4), *Hansel and Gretel* (4), *Jack and the Beanstalk* (5), and *Little Red Riding Hood* (6).

Her feature film credits are: *Hollywood* (4), *The Darling of New York* (4), *The Law Forbids* (5), *Family Secret* (5), *Captain January* (5), *Helen's Babies* (6), and *April Fool* (7).

By the time she was five, Baby Peggy had earned $200,000. In 1926 Peggy undertook a vaudeville tour of the Interstate Circuit that netted her an additional $50,000. Her schooling was accomplished via private tutors.

In the mid-thirties Peggy attempted a comeback in motion pictures but received only a few small roles. She retired to a ranch in Wyoming where, under the name of Diana Cary, she wrote stories for *Esquire* and *Saturday Evening Post.* In the 1960s she was in the process of writing a book concerning her years in motion pictures and vaudeville.

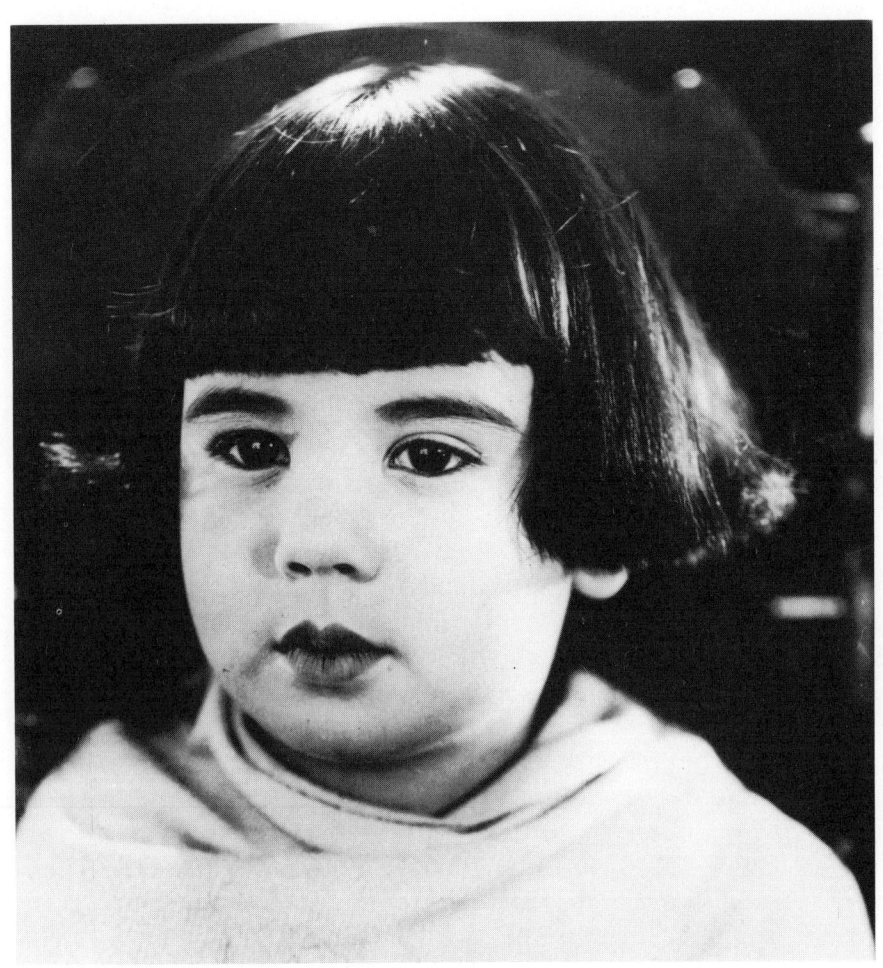

The Darling of New York
(Universal, 1923)

In her first starring role, Baby Peggy appeared as an orphan named Santussa. The picture related her adventures with a rag doll that, unknown to her, carried a fortune in diamonds in its torso. Victor McLaglen also starred.

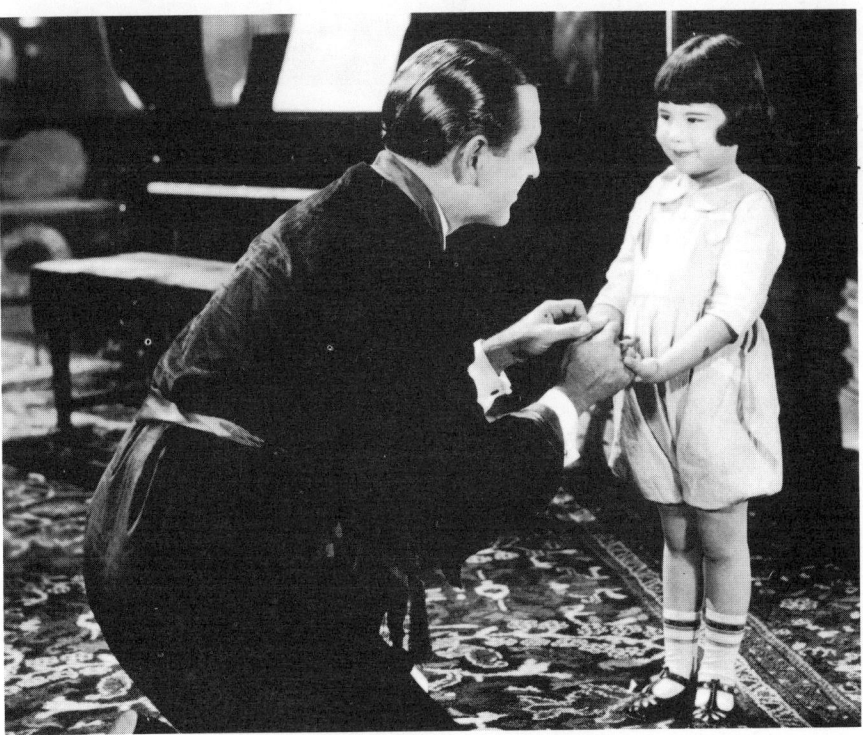

The Law Forbids
(Universal, 1924)

Peggy reunited Robert Ellis and Elinor Fair in this melodrama of marital strife.

The Family Secret
(Universal, 1924)

Captain January
(Principal, 1924)

Here Baby Peggy was seen with Hobart Bosworth in a film about a lighthouse keeper and his diminutive charge, "Star."

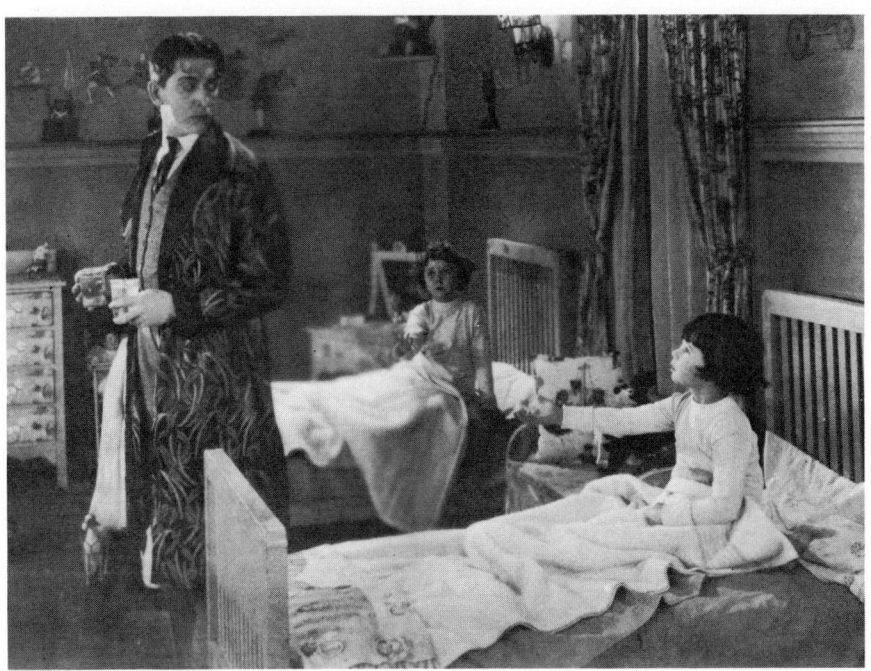

Helen's Babies
(Principal, 1925)

Sol Lesser directed this Baby Peggy film that featured Edward Everett Horton as a writer on child upbringing. Mayhem developed when Horton baby-sat for Peggy and her sister.

JUANITA QUIGLEY
(BABY JANE)

BORN: June 24, 1931. PLACE OF BIRTH: Los Angeles, California. HAIR: Brown. EYES: Hazel.

Juanita and her mother were strolling down Hollywood's Sunset Boulevard one morning in the summer of 1934 when a talent scout stopped them to inquire if the little girl was under contract. Casting officials from Universal Pictures sought a toddler who could handle a significant role in the production *Imitation of Life*. The film scout was impressed with the moppet and felt certain that with the proper training she could become a talented actress. Mrs. Quigley decided on a movie career for her daughter the evening after the chance meeting. Juanita thus became Universal's youngest star earning a salary of $200 to $1000 a week.

On the screen she was in *Imitation of Life* (3), *The Man Who Reclaimed His Head* (3), *Straight From the Heart* (3), *Alias Mary Dow* (3), *Riffraff* (4), *The Devil Doll* (4), *Born To Dance* (5), *Hawaii Calls* (6), *The Devil's Party* (6), *Woman Against Woman* (6), *Having Wonderful Time* (6), *That Certain Age* (7), *Men With Wings* (7), *The Mad Miss Manton* (7), *Code of the Streets* (7), *The Family Next Door* (7), *The Blue Bird* (8), *Oh Johnny, How You Can Love* (8), *The New Pupil* (8), *Bachelor Daddy* (9), *The Vanishing Virginian* (10), *Going To Press* (10), *A Yank At Eaton* (11), *Assignment In Brittany* (11), *The Happy Land* (12), *The Lady and the Monster* (12), and *National Velvet* (13).

Juanita attended dancing school and played the piano in her spare time. She was born to nonprofessional parents, but had a sister, Rita, who acted, on occasion, for MGM.

In 1942 Juanita Quigley left a promising film career for the religious life. Taking her vows in the order of the Daughters of Mary and Joseph, Juanita became Sister Quentin Rita. Her intention was to be a grade-school teacher.

Straight from the Heart
(Universal, 1935)

Juanita had a major part in this feature opposite Mary Astor.

Riffraff
(Metro-Goldwyn-Mayer, 1935)

In this film about the lives of tuna fishermen Spencer Tracy and Jean Harlow had the lead roles. Juanita, pictured here with Miss Harlow, co-starred as Rosie.

Woman Against Woman
(Metro-Goldwyn-Mayer, 1938)

In this film of a domestic triangle Juanita is featured as Mary Astor's daughter.

That Certain Age
(Universal, 1938)

Deanna Durbin headed the cast in this film portraying the daughter of a wealthy newspaper owner. Jackie Cooper starred as Deanna's boyfriend, and Juanita plays Cooper's little sister—"the Pest."

The Family Next Door
(Universal, 1939)

In this film Juanita portrayed the young daughter of a zany couple, played by Hugh Herbert and Ruth Donnelly.

MICHEL RAY

BORN: 1945. PLACE OF BIRTH: Gerrard Cross, Buckingham, England. HAIR: Light brown. EYES: Deep blue.

After an exhaustive search by RKO director Irving Rapper and his producer Maurice King, Michel Ray reached screen stardom. Children in Spain, France, and Italy were tested for the pivotal role in *The Brave One,* but the two men did not find their boy until they attended a private filming of *The Divided Heart.* Michel was flown to the United States and then to Mexico for on-location filming.

Michel was born just a short distance from London, the only child of Mr. and Mrs. Henry Popper of German-French ancestry. His father was not a performer, but his mother had trained to be an opera singer and had studied drama at the Reinhardt School in Vienna. Before his screen debut, Michel's dramatic training had been limited to plays and poetry readings at public school. Later he became a student of the Lycee Francais in Kensington, England, a private school where many professional children received their education. He was an extremely bright youngster who had a sound knowledge of English, French, and German.

Michel's parents harbored no thoughts of a theatrical career for their son until a British film director approached them in early 1955. The director, Charles Crichton, sought a ten-year-old boy who could speak both German and English *and* who was an expert skier. Michel could speak both languages fluently and had won medals in skiing, so it was only fitting that he be chosen for the part in *The Divided Heart.*

In his spare time Michel enjoyed playing the piano. His favorite sports were rugby and skiing. He also spent many of his spare moments collecting stamps and tropical fish.

For his performance in *The Tin Star,* Michel won *Film Daily's* Critics Award and was one of the top ten juvenile performers for 1957.

His film credits are: *The Divided Heart* (10), *The Brave One* (11), *The Tin Star* (12), *Flood Tide* (12), and *The Space Children* (13).

The Divided Heart
(Republic, 1955)

Charles Crichton directed this British film about a war orphan (Michel) who is raised by German foster parents. Cornell Borchers starred as the boy's foster mother.

The Brave One
(RKO Radio, 1956)

Michel starred in this film of a Mexican boy and his affections for a pet bull.

The Brave One
(RKO Radio, 1956)

In this scene Michel watches anxiously as his pet fights for life in the bullring at Mexico City.

The Tin Star
(Paramount, 1957)

This western drama featured Henry Fonda as a bounty hunter who settles down in the home of a widow and her half-breed son. Betsy Palmer and Michel Ray starred as mother and son.

The Space Children
(Paramount, 1958)

A group of children at a rocket base in the Pacific discover a gelatinous mass from outer space. In this scene Michel Ray points out the "thing," which has come to earth to prevent the launching of a hydrogen rocket.

GENE REYNOLDS

BORN: April 4, 1925. PLACE OF BIRTH: Cleveland, Ohio. HAIR: Brown. EYES: Hazel.

Gene Blumenthal, alias Gene Reynolds, had the most publicized face outside of filmdom. He posed for commercial posters, advertisements, and commercial movies from the time he was two years old. The youngster appeared in several films for the Chicago World's Fair and made many advertisements for Standard Oil and General Motors.

Making his acting debut at the age of six, Gene had a role in a Detroit play entitled *We Think We Can*. During the early part of 1936, a film scout viewed one of Gene's commercial shorts and was greatly impressed. The young thespian was soon on his way to Hollywood and a screen career. He undertook a number of tests, then landed a bit role in the Paramount feature *Too Many Parents*.

His film credits are: *Sins of Man* (11), *Thank You, Jeeves* (11), *The Californians* (12), *Thunder Trail* (12), *In Old Chicago* (12), *Of Human Hearts* (12), *Love Finds Andy Hardy* (13), *The Crowd Roars* (13), *Boys Town* (13), *The Spirit of Culver* (13), *The Flying Irishman* (13), *They Shall Have Music* (14), *Bad Little Angel* (14), *The Blue Bird* (14).

Gene Reynolds is currently active in show business as the co-producer of television's "M.A.S.H." series.

In Old Chicago
(20th Century-Fox, 1938)

In this picture of the Chicago fire and its supposed origin—Mother O'Leary's cow—Gene Reynolds had the role of Dion O'Leary as a boy. Gene is pictured here with his mother (Alice Brady) and his two younger brothers as they drive their covered wagon westward across the plains.

Of Human Hearts
(Metro-Goldwyn-Mayer, 1938)

Clarence Brown directed this epic film about the hardships endured by a rugged frontier family named Wilkins. Gene had the part of Jason.

The Crowd Roars
(Metro-Goldwyn-Mayer, 1938)

This film deals with the life of an ex-vaudevillian and his young son, Tommy. Gene played opposite Frank Morgan.

They Shall Have Music
(United Artists, 1939)

For this picture Gene appeared in a starring role as a street urchin named Frankie, who is adopted by the counselor of a settlement music school. Jascha Heifetz, world-famous violinist, is seen in a cameo role.

Bad Little Angel
(Metro-Goldwyn-Mayer, 1939)

In this picture Gene befriends a runaway orphan and finds her a home with the town's newspaper editor. Reginald Owen, Guy Kibbee, and Virginia Weidler co-starred. The film was adapted from the Margaret Turnbull story, "Looking After Sandy."

LARRY SIMMS (BABY DUMPLING)

BORN: October 1, 1934. PLACE OF BIRTH: Los Angeles, California. HAIR: Blond. EYES: Blue.

Larry Simms was the son of singer Margaret Lawrence, who performed with several nightclub bands in the Los Angeles area. Larry was employed as a model before making his acting debut, but did not attain much recognition until 1938 when he became the cover child on an issue of the *Saturday Evening Post*.

Columbia Pictures required a little boy to play the son of Arthur Lake and Penny Singleton in a film based upon the comic strip *Blondie*. Attracted by his cover portrait, studio casting officials decided to test Larry for the part. A long-term contract followed. From the time of his first *Blondie* role late in 1938 until his final one in 1949, Larry Simms performed in a total of twenty-six productions. At first he appeared in the pictures as Baby Dumpling, but later discarded the name and became Alexander.

Early in 1939, soon after his movie debut, Larry was made honorary mayor of the city of Venice, California. His favorite activity was playing the piano.

You can see Larry in these films: *Blondie* (4), *Blondie Meets the Boss* (4), *Blondie Takes a Vacation* (4), *Mr. Smith Goes To Washington* (4), *Blondie Brings Up Baby* (5), *Blondie On a Budget* (5), *Blondie Has Servant Trouble* (5), *Blondie Plays Cupid* (6), *Blondie Goes Latin* (6), *Blondie In Society* (6), *Blondie Goes To College* (7), *Blondie's Blessed Event* (7), *The Gay Sisters* (7), *Blondie for Victory* (7), *It's a Great Life* (8), *Footlight Glamour*

(8), *Leave It To Blondie* (10), *Life With Blondie* (11), *Blondie's Lucky Day* (11), *Blondie Knows Best* (11), *It's a Wonderful Life* (12), *Blondie's Big Moment* (12), *Blondie's Holiday* (12), *Blondie In the Dough* (12), *Blondie's Anniversary* (13), *Blondie's Reward* (13), *Blondie's Secret* (14), *Blondie's Big Deal* (14), *Madame Bovary* (14), *Blondie Hits the Jackpot* (14).

Blondie
(Columbia Pictures, 1938)

On the eve of his fifth wedding anniversary, Dagwood Bumstead (Arthur Lake) develops financial difficulties, while Baby Dumpling's (Larry) innocent escapades add fuel to the fire.

Blondie Meets the Boss
(Columbia Pictures, 1939)

This episode in the lives of Dagwood and Blondie centers around Dagwood's new boss, J. C. Dithers. Larry Simms delivered a few precious lines as the Bumsteads' highchair philosopher-son.

Blondie Goes Latin
(Columbia Pictures, 1941)

The Bumsteads find themselves on a South American cruise in this feature. Mr. Dithers accompanies the family on the tour in hopes of recuperating from a long illness. Jonathan Hale portrayed J. C. Dithers and Penny Singleton was Blondie.

Blondie's Blessed Event
(Columbia Pictures, 1942)

Frank Strayer directed most of the Blondie films, which were based upon the comic-strip character created by Chic Young. Larry Simms was seen in every film in the series.

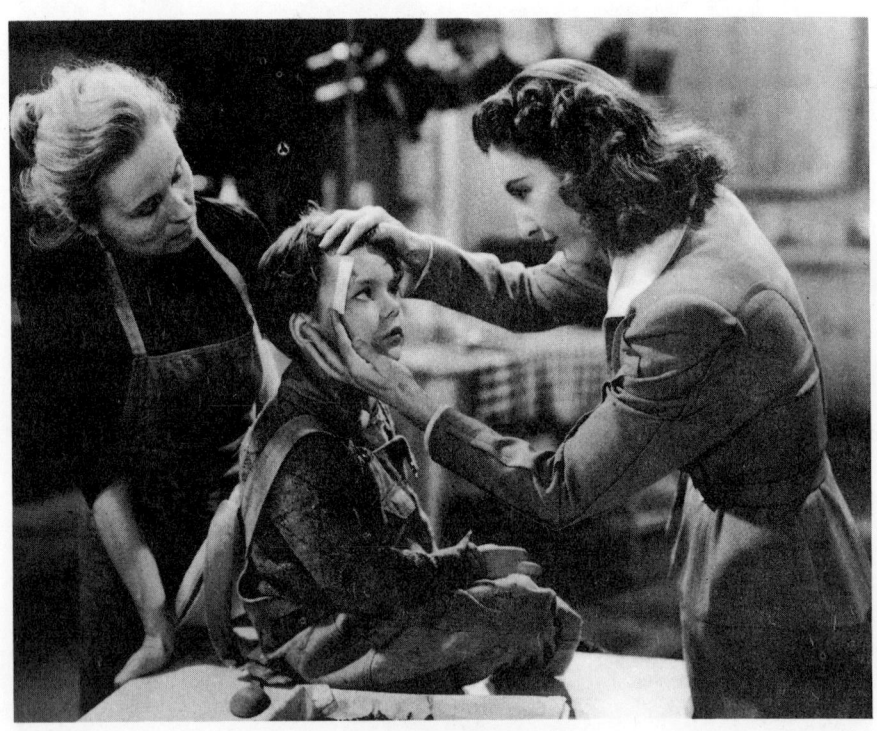

The Gay Sisters
(Warner Brothers, 1942)

Larry appeared as a member of an eccentric family named Gaylord in this film-caricature starring Barbara Stanwyck.

ELIZABETH TAYLOR

BORN: February 27, 1932. PLACE OF BIRTH: London, England. HAIR: Black. EYES: Blue.

At the age of three, Elizabeth Taylor was one of a group of dancers who performed in a recital at Queens Hall before Princesses Elizabeth and Margaret Rose. It occurred only a few months after her enrollment in a ballet school run by the famed Vaccani, whose students also included members of the royal family. In 1939 the threat of war in Europe became a certainty, so the girl was sent to live with her grandparents in Pasadena, California.

A year following her arrival in the 'States, Elizabeth became acquainted with J. Cheever Cowdin who secured her a one-year contract with Universal Pictures. Even though she had fine singing abilities and was trained in the musical arts for a full year, Elizabeth made only one film for the studio. The film, *There's One Born Every Minute* (9), saw her perform a duet with the long-time *Our Gang* member Carl "Alfalfa" Switzer.

Early in 1943, an MGM executive named Samuel Marx approached Francis Taylor to inquire if Elizabeth was available for a movie role. Mr. Taylor replied affirmatively and his daughter was subsequently cast as a British girl in the film *Lassie Come Home* (11). Her other film assignments were: *Jane Eyre* (11), *The White Cliffs of Dover* (11), *National Velvet* (12), and *Courage of Lassie* (14).

Elizabeth adored animals and she owned a wide variety of pets that included a chipmunk named "Nibbles" and a horse named "Peanuts." Her favorite pastime was horseback riding, which she undertook at the age of four.

In England the moppet was schooled at the Byron House, but her education in the United States came through the Hawthorne School in Beverly Hills and the MGM Studio School, which was also known as "the Little Red Schoolhouse." Elizabeth was a talented little actress. She received the *Film Daily* Critics Award for *National Velvet* and *Courage of Lassie* and she delivered one of the top five performances by a juvenile actress for 1944 and 1946, respectively.

One of Elizabeth's most cherished moments came during the Christmas season of 1944, shortly after her film *National Velvet* began to be shown in theaters around the country. It was then that she was invited to have tea at the White House with the First Lady, Eleanor Roosevelt.

Lassie Come Home
(Metro-Goldwyn-Mayer, 1943)

Eric Knight's novel about an impoverished family and their prize collie is brought to the screen with Roddy McDowall and Elizabeth Taylor featured. McDowall played Lassie's young master and Elizabeth was seen as his girlfriend, Priscilla. In picture are Elizabeth, Elsa Lanchester, Donald Crisp, and Nigel Bruce.

Jane Eyre
(20th Century-Fox, 1944)

Charlotte Bronte's novel brought to the screen starred Joan Fontaine in the title role as an adult, while Peggy Ann Garner played Jane Eyre as a child. The film told of Jane's life in an orphanage and of her friendship with Helen, a frail little girl who was to die needlessly from pneumonia. Elizabeth portrayed the girl, Helen.

The White Cliffs of Dover
(Metro-Goldwyn-Mayer, 1944)

In this picture Elizabeth played a charming youngster named Betsy, who falls in love with an English nobleman's son (Roddy McDowall). The film was directed by Clarence Brown and was based on the poem by Alice Duer Miller.

National Velvet
(Metro-Goldwyn-Mayer, 1944)

Elizabeth appeared as an English girl, the daughter of a butcher, who trains a gelding to run in the Grand National Steeplechase. Clarence Brown directed and Mickey Rooney co-starred.

Courage of Lassie
(Metro-Goldwyn-Mayer, 1946)

Lassie starred in this picture as an Army K-9 dog who is injured during World War II. Suffering from shock, the dog is reunited with its mistress (Elizabeth) and restored to health through her love.

REX THOMPSON

BORN: December 14, 1942. PLACE OF BIRTH: New York City. HAIR: Brown. EYES: Brown.

Rex Thompson gave evidence of acting talents at a very early age. John Thompson, a onetime actor, recognized his son's latent abilities and coached him in the dramatic arts. As soon as he felt his son was ready to accept an assignment, Mr. Thompson procured him a role on the Broadway stage in *Alive and Kicking* (7). Opening at the Winter Garden Theatre, the play was a musical review that featured Rex and an all-star cast headed by Bobby Van and Carl Reiner.

A year following his stage debut, Rex did a few performances of *The King and I* on Broadway. He was noticed by talent scouts from MGM and signed to a multi-year pact at a starting salary of $500 a week. From that moment on the youngster was in constant demand for acting appearances, shuttling back and forth between Hollywood and New York.

In addition to the aforementioned Broadway plays, Rex also performed in *Escapade* (10) and *King of Hearts* (11). His film assignments were: *Young Bess* (10), *Her Twelve Men* (11), *The Eddy Duchin Story* (13), *The King and I* (13), *All Mine To Give* (14). Rex also acted on the small screen. He appeared in "Robert Montgomery Presents" (11), "Center Stage" (11), "TV Playhouse" (11), "TV Theater" (12), "Omnibus" (12), "Kaiser Aluminum Hour" (13), "Studio One" (14), and "Dupont Show of the Month" (14).

While appearing on the stage, Rex received his schooling at the Professional Children's School. In Hollywood he was educated by a private tutor. His hobby was photography and his favorite sport was baseball.

In 1954 Rex was the recipient of the Yale University Award as the outstanding child actor of the year. Two years later he won the Critics Award for *The Eddy Duchin Story* and was voted by *Film Daily* as giving one of the ten best performances by a juvenile performer.

Young Bess
(Metro-Goldwyn-Mayer, 1953)

Jean Simmons starred in this film that depicts the early years of Queen Elizabeth. Rex played the sickly King Edward.

Her Twelve Men
(Metro-Goldwyn-Mayer, 1954)

For this film Rex played Homer Curtis, a rich boy in a rather prim boarding school. Greer Garson starred in the role of an inexperienced housemother.

The Eddy Duchin Story
(Columbia Pictures, 1956)

In this biographical film of the dance-band pianist, Eddy Duchin, Tyrone Power was seen in the leading role, while Rex Thompson portrayed his son, Peter.

The King and I
(20th Century-Fox, 1956)

In this film depicting the relationship between an English schoolteacher named Anna and her employer, the King of Siam, Rex co-starred as Anna's son, Louis. Deborah Kerr and Yul Brynner were seen in the main roles.

All Mine to Give
(Universal, 1957)

Following the death of his parents, a young boy named Robbie sets out on Christmas Day to locate homes for his four brothers and sisters. Rex is shown here "delivering" his sister, Elizabeth.

ANN TODD

BORN: August 26, 1932. PLACE OF BIRTH: Denver, Colorado. HAIR: Golden brown. EYES: Brown.

At the age of four Ann Todd Mayfield was modeling for a number of department stores in her hometown. Her earliest professional acting experience occurred when she was five, performing in a church play in Longmont, Colorado. Ann's parents moved to the West Coast with no intention of entering their daughter in pictures, but fate decided otherwise. On the day in which she took part in a church play, *The Gift,* a Dorothy McDonald was in attendance. Miss McDonald, a teacher at the Los Angeles Manual Arts High School, doubled as a part-time agent, and she felt Ann had the necessary credentials for a movie career. With her help Ann obtained an interview with George Cukor, a Paramount director, who had the youngster cast in *Zaza.* She had only a brief role as Herbert Marshall's daughter, but this was more than enough to convince everyone of her acting capabilities.

Zaza (6), was followed by: *Zero Hour* (6), *Stronger Than Desire* (6), *Intermezzo: A Love Story* (7), *Destry Rides Again* (7), *The Blue Bird* (7), *Little Orvie* (7), *Granny Get Your Gun* (7), *All This, and Heaven Too* (7), *Brigham Young—Frontiersman* (7), *Blood and Sand* (8), *Private Nurse* (8), *Badmen of Missouri* (8), *The Men In Her Life* (9), *How Green Was My Valley* (9), *Kings Row* (9), *Remember the Day* (9), *On the Sunny Side* (9), *Beyond the Blue Horizon* (9), *Dixie Dugan* (10), *Roughly Speaking* (12), *Pride of the Marines* (12), *My Reputation* (13), and **The Jolson Story** (13).

Ann attended the Lawlor Professional School, the **Chermoya** Public School, and the 20th Century-Fox Studio School. She was an extremely bright little girl with an IQ of 146. Besides acting, the moppet occupied her time with voice and piano lessons.

Stronger Than Desire
(Metro-Goldwyn-Mayer, 1939)

In this drama of blackmail and murder, Ann Todd portrayed a criminal lawyer's daughter.

Intermezzo: A Love Story
(United Artists, 1939)

Leslie Howard starred as a famous violinist who falls in love with his daughter's music teacher. Ingrid Bergman played the teacher. **Ann** co-starred as Howard's daughter, with Edna Best as her mother.

Private Nurse
(20th Century-Fox, 1941)

In this film Ann played the sickly daughter of an erstwhile beer baron, Sheldon Leonard.

Remember the Day
(20th Century-Fox, 1941)

Claudette Colbert starred in this heartwarming picture about the life of a simple schoolteacher in a country town. Ann was seen as Kate, one of her young pupils. Douglas Croft also appeared.

Dixie Dugan
(20th Century-Fox, 1943)

This film was adapted from the comic strip created by Joseph McEvoy and starred Lois Andrews as the light-minded secretary. Ann portrayed Dixie's younger sister, Imogene.